Paolo Roversi

Introduction by Chiara Bardelli Nonino

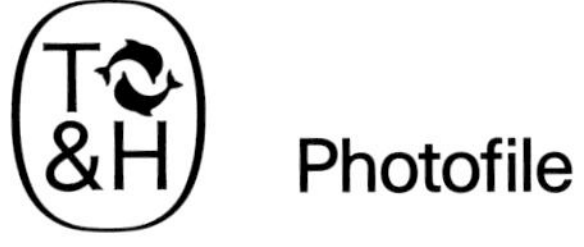

Photofile

Gazing at shadows

In a famous and forthright work of theatrical theory, Peter Brook wrote: 'I can take any empty space and call it a stage A man walks across this empty space whilst someone else is watching him, and this is all that is needed for an act of theatre to be engaged.'' This commitment to a bare and sublimated space is a philosophy that Brook tested out in the field: a year after moving to Paris, the British director began an 8,000-mile tour of Africa in which, every day, in a different remote village, he would lay down a carpet on the ground. As soon as someone stepped on it, the performance began. There was no need for a codified language, or for tricks or costumes: the magic of the creative act took place in absolute simplicity.

The same subtractive process, with everything reduced to its bare essentials, lies at the centre of the practice of one of the greatest Italian photographers: Paolo Roversi. The empty space is the frame around the photograph; the stage is his studio; the carpet is an old military blanket. All that is needed is for someone to walk into that setting, and the ineffable quality that Roversi tries to capture in his work springs into life – an emotion, a kind of illumination. Or perhaps even a small piece of the truth.

At the centre – or perhaps the most appropriate word is heart – of this ritual is the studio: it is there that Roversi manages to create a sense of liberty, a distancing from reality. When the door closes, the world is left outside: everything except the photographer, his subject, and a virtually infinite space for interpretation. For this reason, when asked to describe the poetry behind his work, Roversi always suggests a variation on the theme of absence: the blanket backdrop hanging against a wall, the scratched back of his Deardorff, or the studio itself, with just a pair of shoes lying in the middle of the floor. They may seem like nothing more than evocative images, but in fact they are doorways to the otherworld that Paolo endlessly explores with his photography.

Born in Ravenna in 1947, Roversi claims that he became a fashion photographer by chance. It may be true that the unexpected played a key role in the transformation of this boy from Ravenna, the youngest of five children, a doctor's son with a deep fear of the dark, into one of the most celebrated photographers of his generation, but it is also likely that this happened because Roversi has always practised what he himself calls the very essence of photography: the art of the encounter.

Paolo was given his first camera, an Elioflex Ferrania 4 × 4, at the age of eight, but his photographic story began even earlier. In his little room overlooking the Piazza dell'Aquila, where he saw monsters and heroes dancing on the wall every night, made from shadows and patches of light. Today, he has no doubt that those were his first photographs. Or at least that's what he considers them to be, and it's worth taking him at his word.

In fact, Roversi has always seen his relationship with the technical aspects of photography as secondary: far more important is the ability to speak with light, to understand its modulations, its whims. As for the rest, Paolo has always allowed himself the luxury of being grammatically – and even intentionally – incorrect. If the Elioflex manual told him to always take photographs with the sun behind him, he immediately started to take pictures facing the sun. And because the manual stated a mininum distance but gave no maximum distance, Paolo began believing that with that little camera he could photograph far beyond the sea, out into the invisible.

In his early photographic experiments, Paolo sought help from the local postman, Battista Minguzzi. Later, still in Ravenna, he began an apprenticeship in the studio of photographer Nevio Natali. He shot some interesting photo stories – on the work of the then-huge Living Theatre, then on Ezra Pound's funeral – but almost immediately realized that this was not the path for him.

In 1971, at the home of a family friend, he met Peter Knapp, then art director of *Elle*. Knapp looked at his pictures, put them on the floor, rearranged their order, and suddenly Roversi glimpsed a world where photography was not limited to recording reality: it could sing, reveal, narrate. From that meeting – a chance encounter – Roversi came away with one fixed goal in mind: Paris.

Roversi arrived in Paris in 1973, and his first shoot said a lot about his future choices. From the countless subjects available, Paolo opted for one of the places that has helped to shape the modern myth of the city: he went to the English-language bookstore Shakespeare & Company, in Saint Germain, and pointed a Hasselblad – always without a flash – at the customers wandering among the shelves or leafing through the books. The final images were hopelessly out of focus, but after developing them, Paolo not only decided that this was how they were meant to be, but also coined a name for them. He decided to present them as 'Roversi's famous blurry pictures'. It was a joke, but only up to a point: the fuzziness, faults and imperfections instantly became the most recognizable, as well as the most innovative, characteristics of his style.

As far as photography was concerned, and fashion photography in particular, Paris in those years was quite simply the centre of the world. Magazines were packed with images by Newton, Bourdin, Avedon and Penn; young photographers like Peter Lindbergh and Steve Hiett were working in the city; and the editor-in-chief of *Marie Claire* was Claude Brouet, who would leave her own distinctive and lasting mark on the editorial style of the times. To Roversi, she became a true mentor.

Following a brief period working as an assistant to Laurence Sackman – an extraordinary but moody artist, who made an indelible impression with his cardinal rule of keeping the tripod stable and letting the mind fly free – Roversi began to familiarize himself with the world of fashion and its leading figures: editors, photographers, designers. He was, and always remained, a self-taught photographer, and he learned the hidden complexities of that strange and glittering realm on the job. But he now knew what he wanted to photograph, and how to do it.

After a few still lifes and some early jobs for *Depeche Mode*, *Elle* and
Marie Claire, the fateful encounter occurred – and it was with a brand
of film that was different from all the rest. In 1980, at the Pin-Up
studio on the avenue Jean Moulin, Roversi went to a presentation of
the Polaroid 8 × 10, alongside other photographers. It was a revelation.
Not even a week later, in New York, he bought the large-format
Deardorff that he still uses today. For much of his career, it would
be his artist's palette.

It was a sudden revelation, but in many ways not so surprising.
Roversi is perhaps the contemporary artist most closely bound to the
materiality of photography, to the craftsmanship of the act and the
tactility of the image, and working with the large-format Polaroid
meant rediscovering photography's original techniques and emotions:
rather like making a daguerrotype today. Roversi is a very cultured
photographer, and at the same time a believer in wonder. He is
always seeking out a certain kind of light, always trying to recapture
it: the light that enchanted him as a child, in the shadowy basilica
of Sant'Apollinare, and which he thought could be perceived in the
studio work of Nadar or Julia Margaret Cameron, in the early days of
photography – when images seemed to have been born on the fine
line between art, science and alchemy.

That is the line that Roversi continues to walk, with the aid of the
Polaroid 8 × 10, building an alternative reality, showing everything
that photographers generally prefer to avoid: blur, craftsmanship,
altered colours, mistakes with contrast. One image at a time, Roversi
takes the outtake aesthetic usually associated with the backstage
realm, or with intimate or family occasions, and makes into his
style signature.

This unmistakeable style is now widely recognized. But back in
the early days, not everybody understood it. For example, when the
designers at *Marie Claire* received Paolo's first editorial shoot for the
magazine, they immediately sent the package back and asked for
the correct prints to be sent instead – they simply couldn't believe
that these were what they already had on the table. But Roversi was
stubborn, and recognition came shortly after, when he used his
8 × 10 to shoot a campaign for Dior Beauté: those close-ups floating

against a milky background and bold and graphic double exposures overcame any doubts.

1981 was an important year: the gravitational field of Paris attracted two young Japanese designers, Yohji Yamamoto and Rei Kawakubo, while Roversi moved into an old studio building in the 14th *arrondissement*, with large north-facing windows that flooded it with light. Paolo quickly filled the space with chairs and stools found out on the street and furniture from his childhood, gave it the meaningful name of Studio Luce – *luce* being Italian for 'light' – and transformed it into a welcoming workshop that's also a place of the mind and an alchemist's laboratory, where it is possible to transform matter into spirit and spirit into matter.

If you put Paolo's back to the wall and asked him which piece of work had the biggest impact on his aesthetic, it's very likely that he would tell the tale of the Yohji Yamamoto catalogue for Autumn–Winter 1985–86. The shoot took place in Brittany, in the open air, with four models. For two days, not a single decent photograph emerged. On the third day, Roversi realized what he really needed, if he was to express himself: his own studio.

So everyone went back to Paris, and all the models were sent home, except one: Sasha Robertson. With the soundtrack to Fellini's 8½ playing in the background, Sasha posed in oversized hats in front of a white backdrop. She was tall, slender and beautiful. Her hands were blue and her face was lit in red. The images were far removed from the mainstream, and in some ways difficult to square with fashion photography in the commonly understood sense, but they immediately caught the eye and refused to let it go. There was a little apprehension about the client's potential reaction, but in fact he was won over immediately, instinctively knowing that those images would endure far beyond a single season.

Roversi often says that he feels like an orchestra conductor, that what he is doing is interpreting, albeit skilfully, a score written by someone else – the designer. Whether or not that is true, it is undeniable that his relationships with designers, particularly the members of the Japanese wave, have been formative. For example, it was while working for Comme des Garçons in 1997 that Paolo began to paint unusual glowing effects with a flashlight: after learning to speak with light, now he understood how to dance with it. His relationship with Rei Kawakubo, meanwhile, is a continuous exchange that happens through materials, colours and volumes, whether on the walls of museums or in the pages of *Dazed* or *Luncheon*.

What Roversi admires most about Japan is the art of nuance, the capacity to pursue a kind of beauty that is elusive and self-contained. Moreover, one of the formative texts for Roversi is *In Praise of Shadows* by Jun'ichirō Tanizaki, in which the writer explains how Japanese society, unlike Western society, developed an idea of beauty that can be born out of shadows: beauty that is hazy and delicate, 'that suggests, evokes, but does not say'.[2]

These rarefied shadows are the very material that Roversi's images are made from. His work is a kind of shadow photography, all ambiguities and omissions, where inner and outer worlds seem to touch for a moment, and the subjects seem to glow with an iridescent light before being swallowed up by darkness. Like Japanese houses, Roversi's images define the boundaries of a shadow world, open to the night, with rooms ready to be filled by our own imaginations.

It's surely strange that this almost mystical attitude to images is manifested in a realm that seems like its complete opposite: fashion. But it is a paradox that's apparent in all of Roversi's work: on one side, an obsessive search for the essence, the soul, the roots of beauty; on the other, an artform that's more concerned than any other with the ephemeral, the present, the fleeting: an artform that's continuously evolving, that measures time in seasons and weeks, whose *raison d'être* is 'the eternal recurrence of the new'.[3] And yet the key to his images can be found precisely in this contrast between time and its absence – or, to use a more obvious comparison, between the profane and the sacred.

The designers that Roversi works with are well aware of these things – as well as Yohji Yamamoto and Rei Kawakubo, they include John Galliano, Romeo Gigli, Azzedine Alaïa and Jean Paul Gaultier, to mention just a few. They have all seen their creations transformed into fragments of form and colour, acquiring new and unexpected meanings. Paolo's models – Kirsten, Natalia, Audrey,

Naomi, Saskia, Molly, Kate, Malgosia, Guinevere – appear as no other photographer can capture them, to the point of acquiring a radical otherness, in a perfect short-circuit between the individual and the universal.

British art historian Martin Harrison once told Paolo Roversi that his photographs were like icons, they resembled the Madonnas of Dante Gabriel Rossetti. At first, Paolo thought the comparison was a little blasphemous. Then, on going back to his parents' house in Ravenna, he suddenly realized where the intense gazes, the frontal poses, the bodies haloed by light in so many of his photographs came from: from the gold and mosaics of Byzantium, which had surrounded him in his childhood.

The comparison is almost obvious – but in this particular case, virtually unavoidable. Although perhaps, digging a little deeper, the true roots of Roversi's images lie in the Italian poetry of the 20th century: Giuseppe Ungaretti, Salvatore Quasimodo, and most of all Eugenio Montale – his silent, twilight world where an image suddenly surges into view: 'the disappearing horizon, where the light of a petrol tanker occasionally blinks'.[4] Meaning in Roversi's photographs is like the light from that ship: a sudden, intermittent glow, concealed at the edge of the frame. His images exist in doubt and uncertainty, poised on the border between two worlds. It is no surprise that Franca Sozzani, the legendary editor of *Vogue Italia* with whom Roversi collaborated until the end of her life, called on Paolo whenever she wanted to capture the dream, the fantasy, the otherworldliness of fashion.

Roversi is an artist who eludes definitions and detests labels. Perhaps this is why he chose to express himself through fashion: to continue his quest for the absolute, without being forced to provide explanations. To use fiction to search for fragments of reality. Behind the haze and graininess, the dark and opaline splendour, his images are often extremely clear, all too much so. When we learn to look at them, they tell us that when confronted by mystery, there is only one thing to do: contemplate its beauty, in silence.

Chiara Bardelli Nonino

Notes

1   Peter Brook, *The Empty Space: A Book About the Theatre*, New York: Atheneum, 1968.

2   Adriana Boscaro, foreword to Jun'ichiro Tanizaki, *Libro d'ombra* (Italian edition of In Praise of Shadows), Milan: Bompiani, 2022.

3   Walter Benjamin, 'Central Park' (1938–39), in *Selected Writings*, vol. 4, ed. Michael W. Jennings, Cambridge, MA: Harvard University Press, 2003.

4   Eugenio Montale, 'La casa dei doganieri', in *La casa dei doganieri e altri versi*, Florence: Vallechi Editore, 1932.

1. Blanket, Paris, 2002.

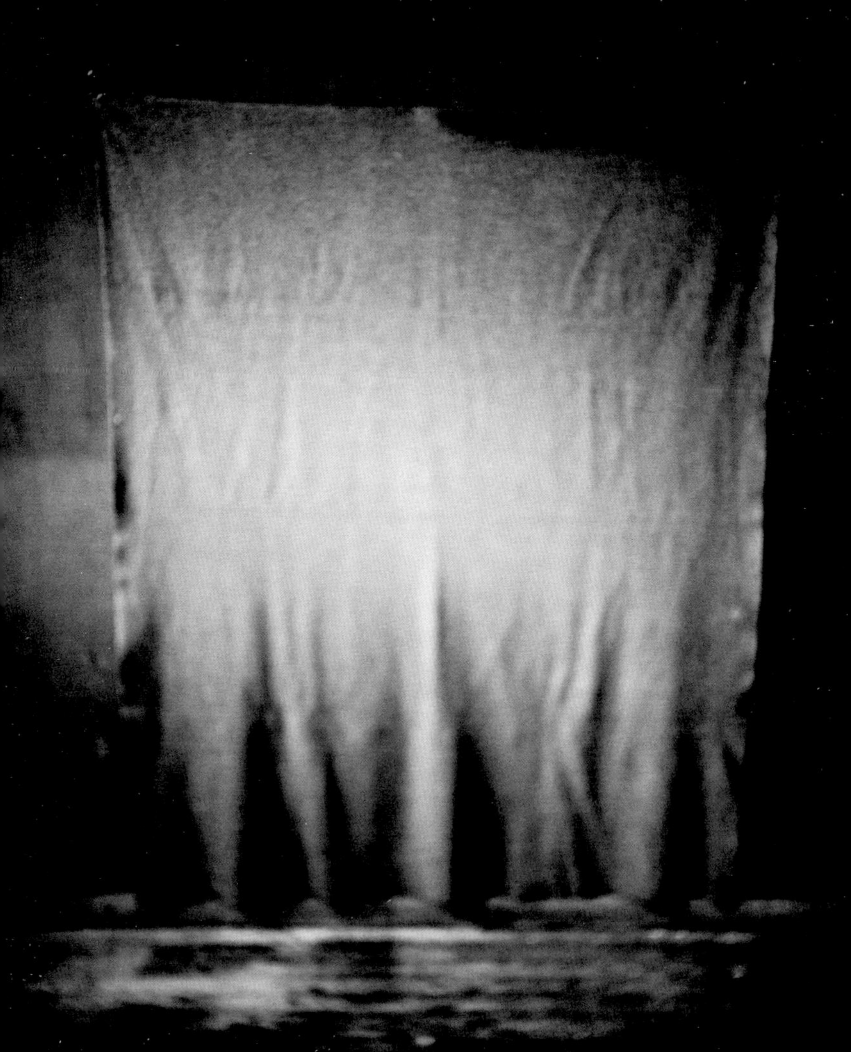

2. Kate, New York, 1993.

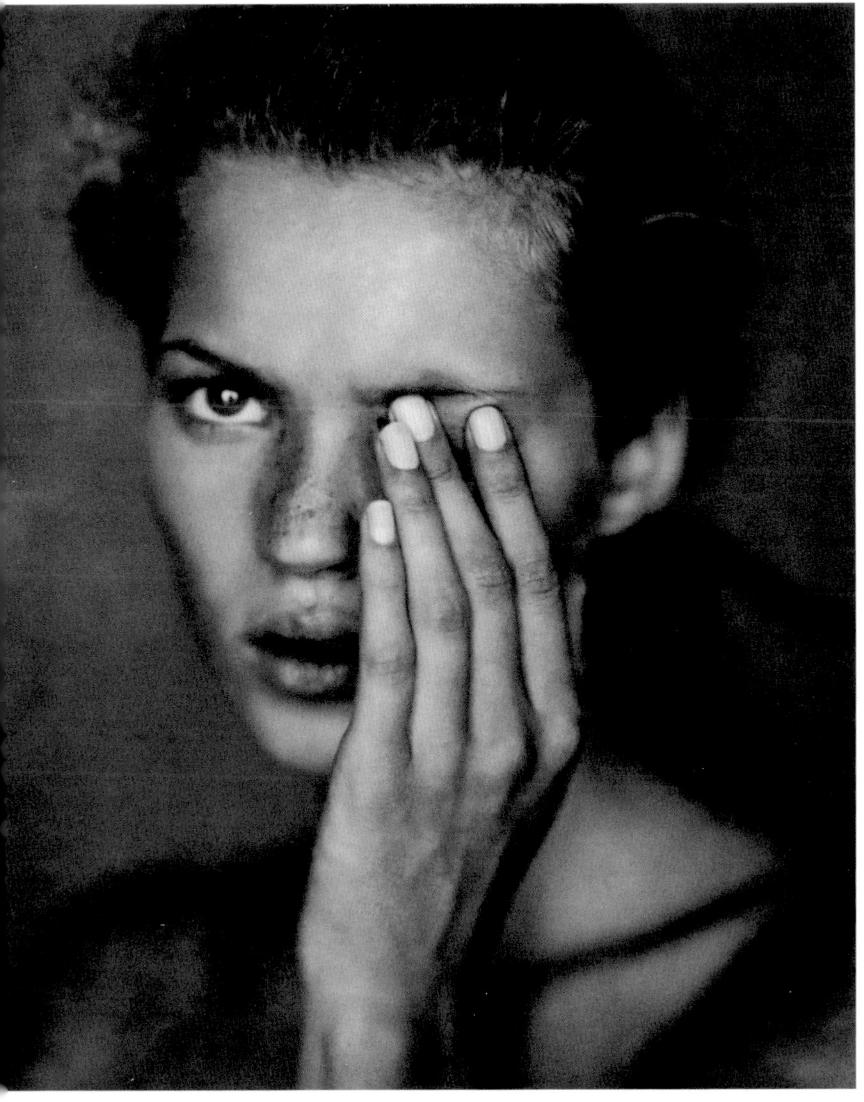

3. Lens, Paris, 2002.

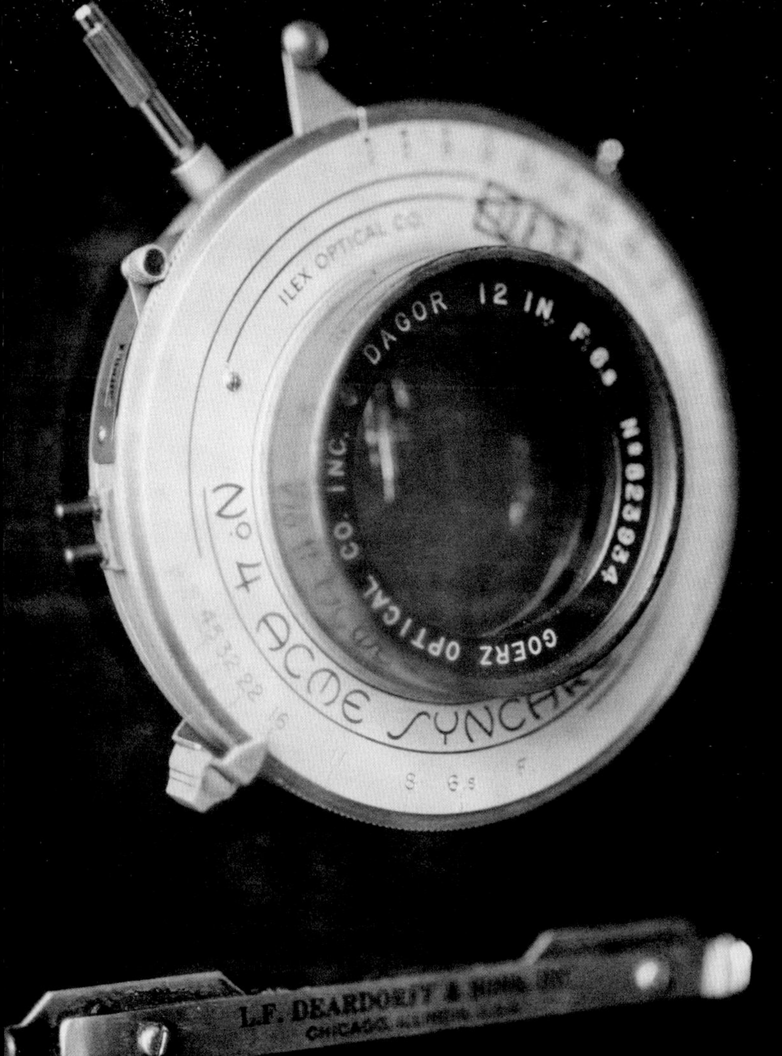

4. Kirsten, London, 1988.

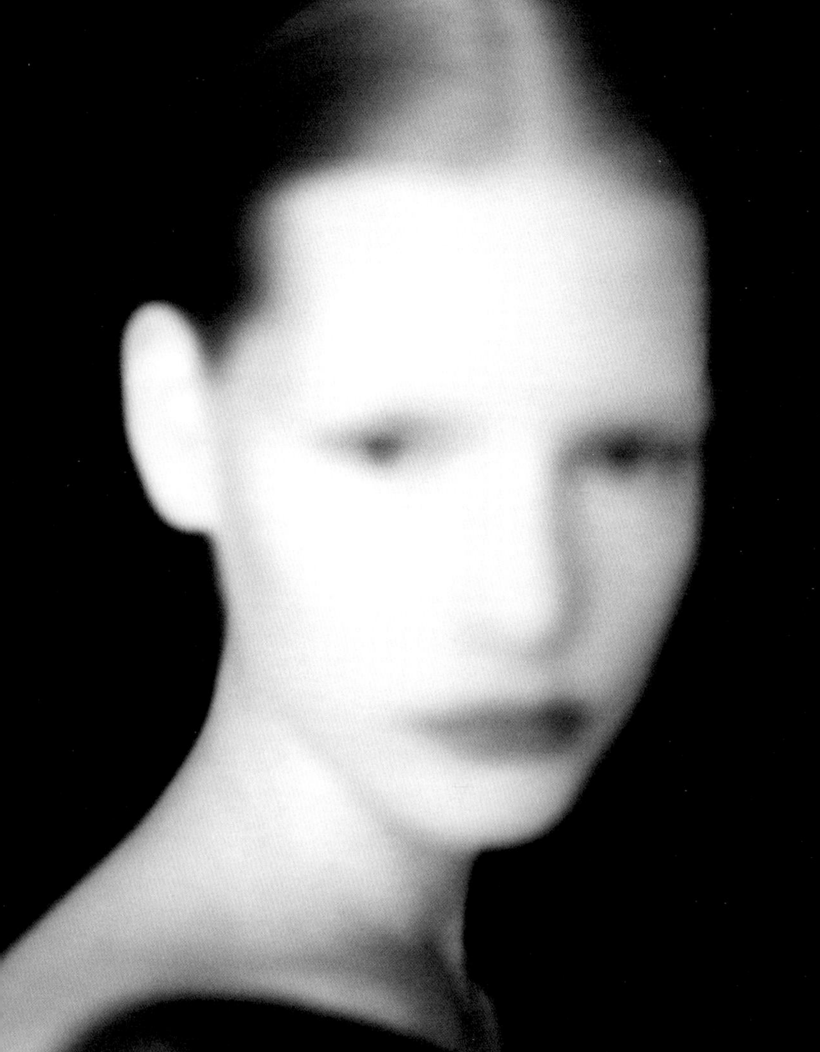

5. Natalia, Paris, 2003.

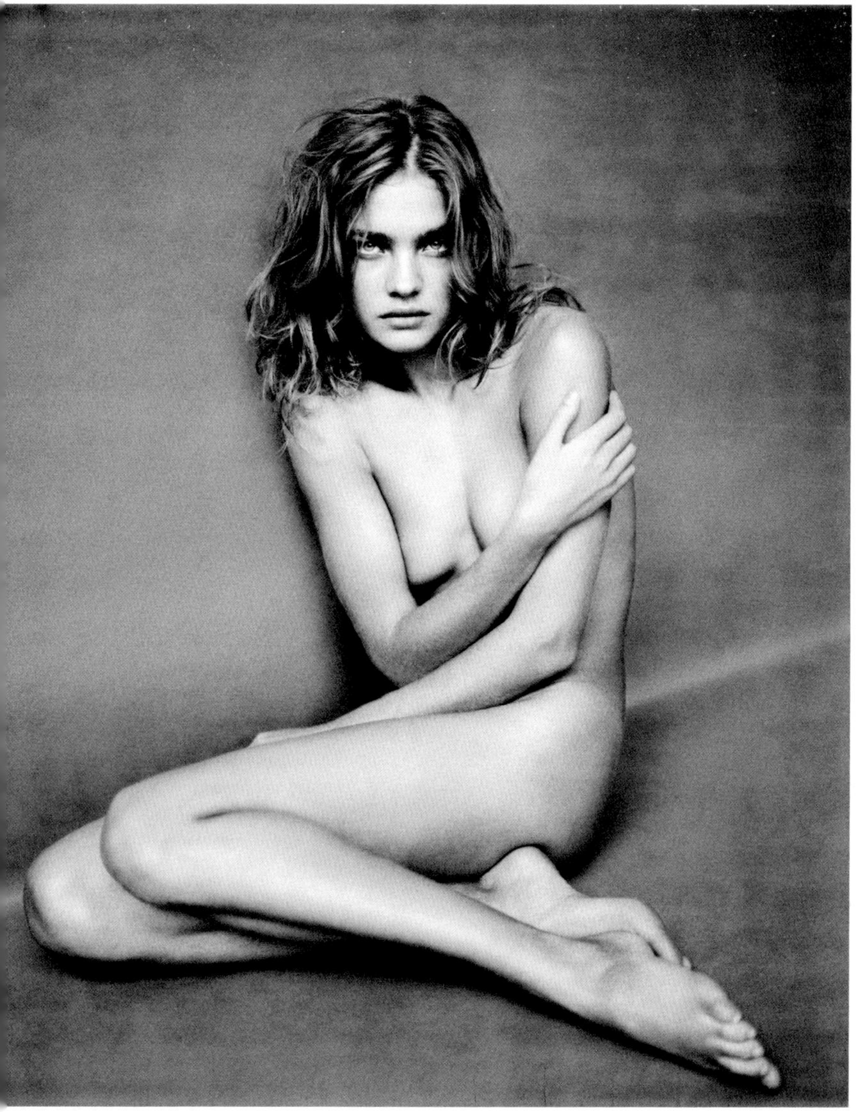

6. Natalia, Paris, 2003.

Overleaf:
7. Bellows, Paris, 2002.
8. Daria, Paris, 2008.

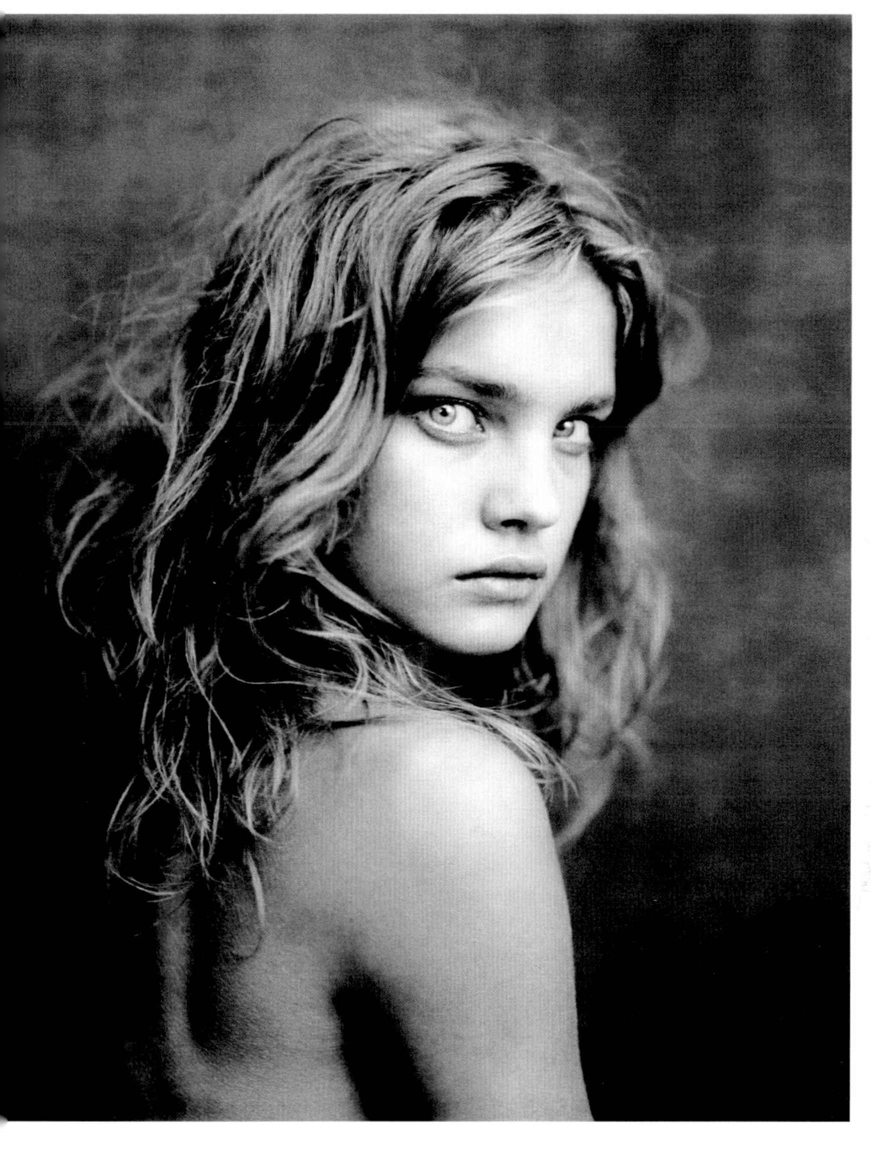

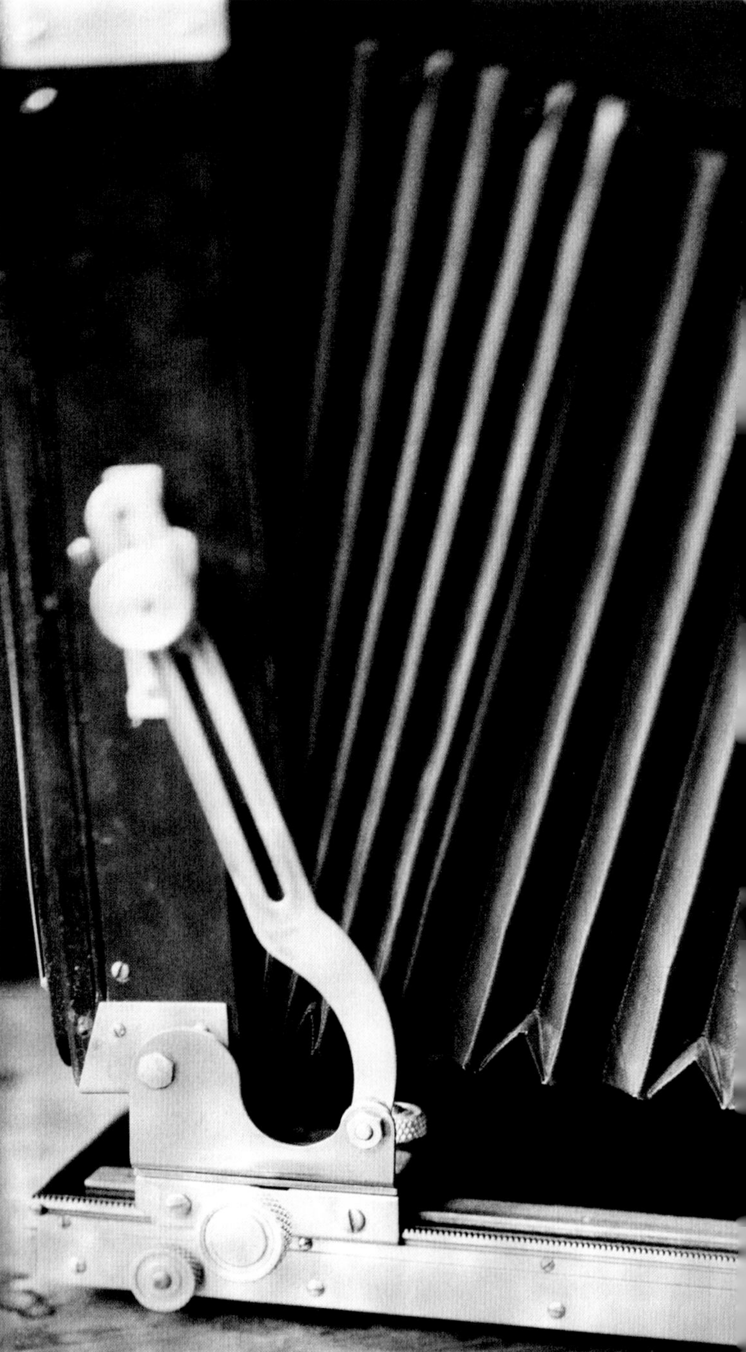

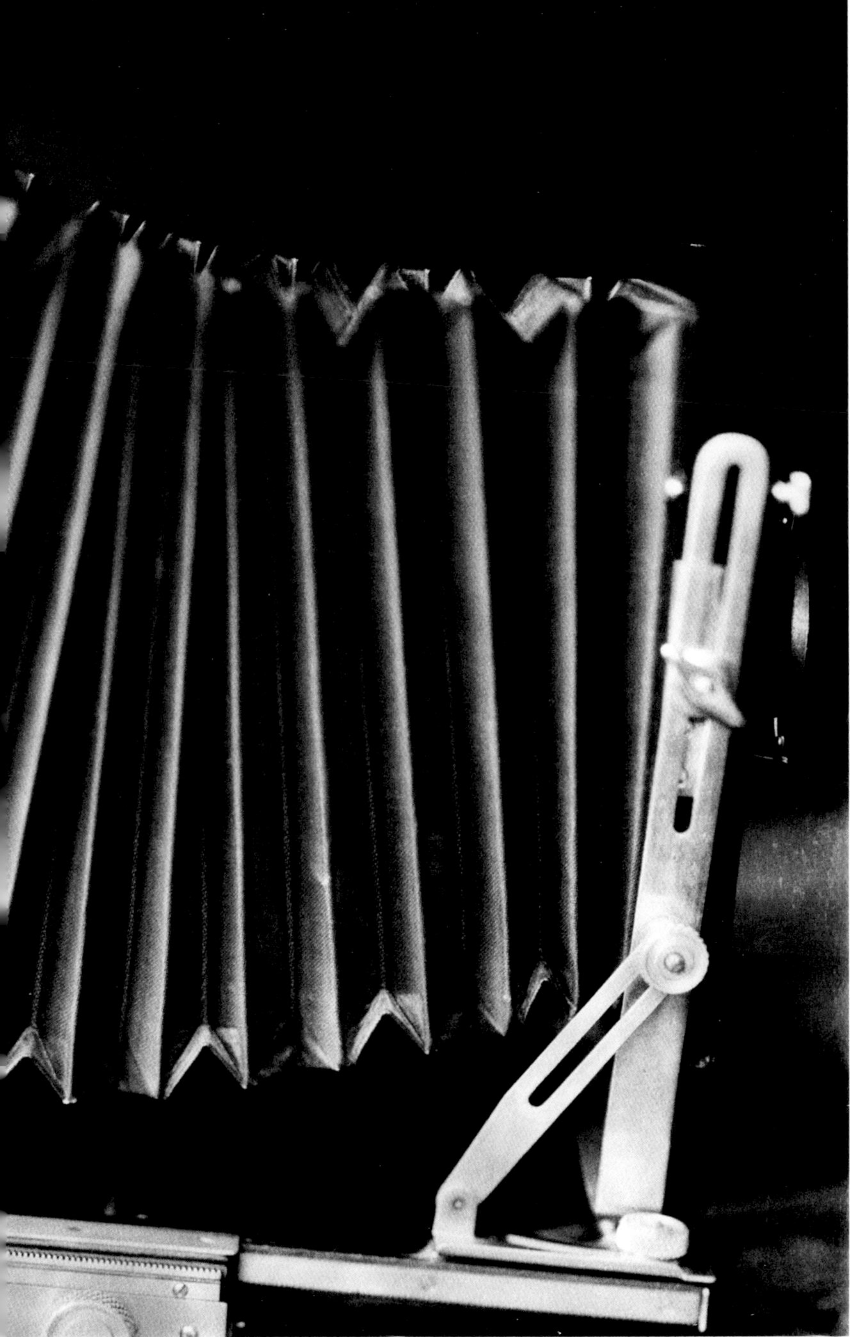

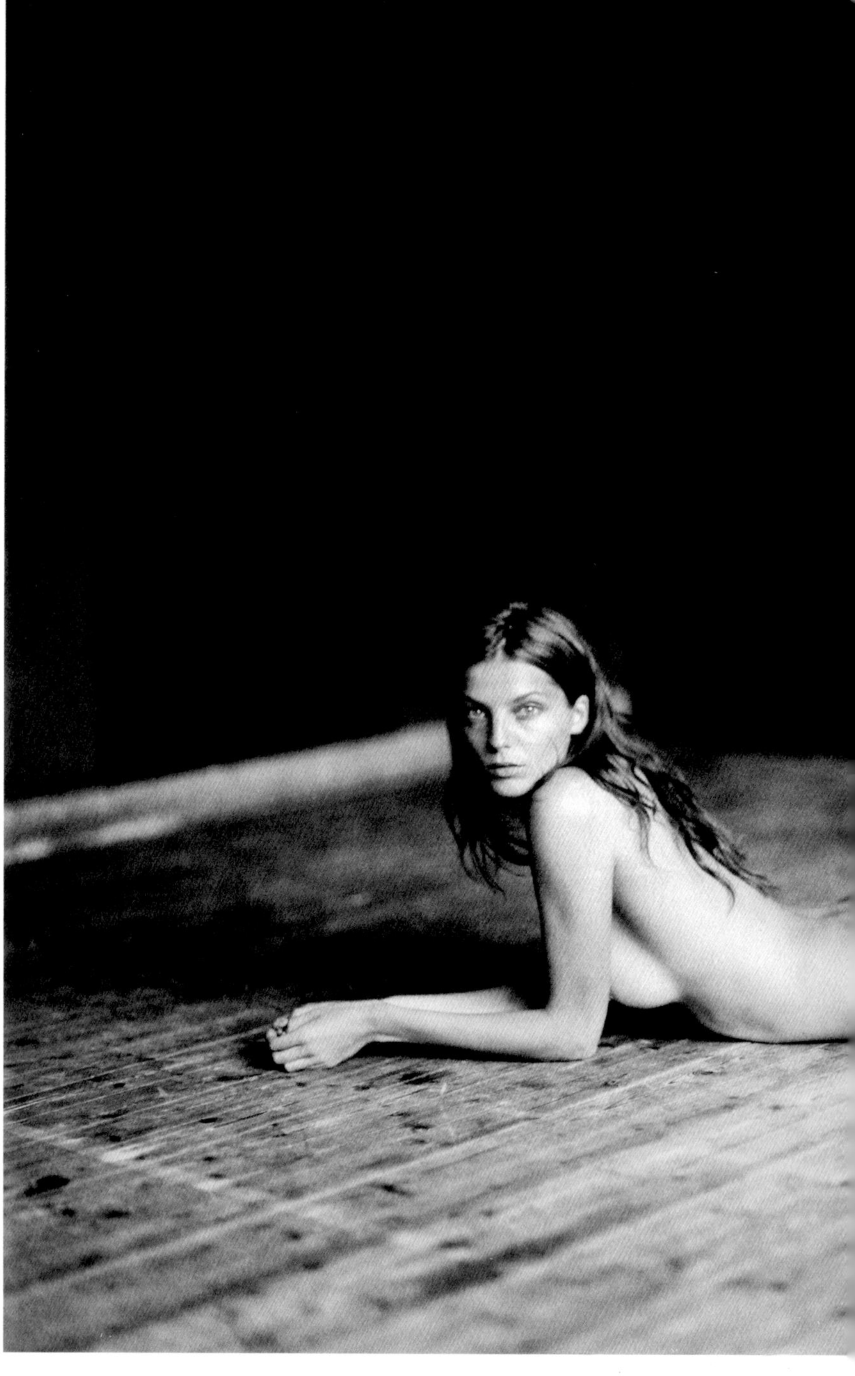

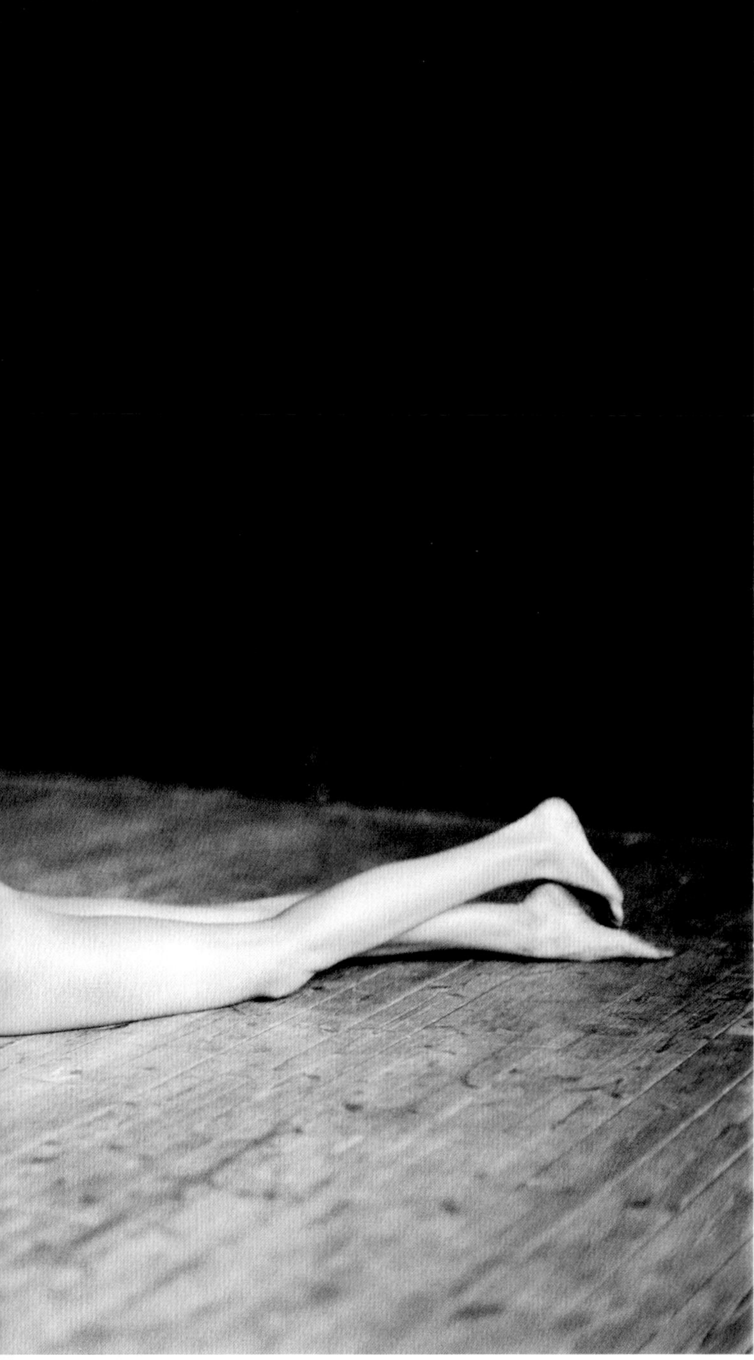

9. Lucie, Paris, 1990.

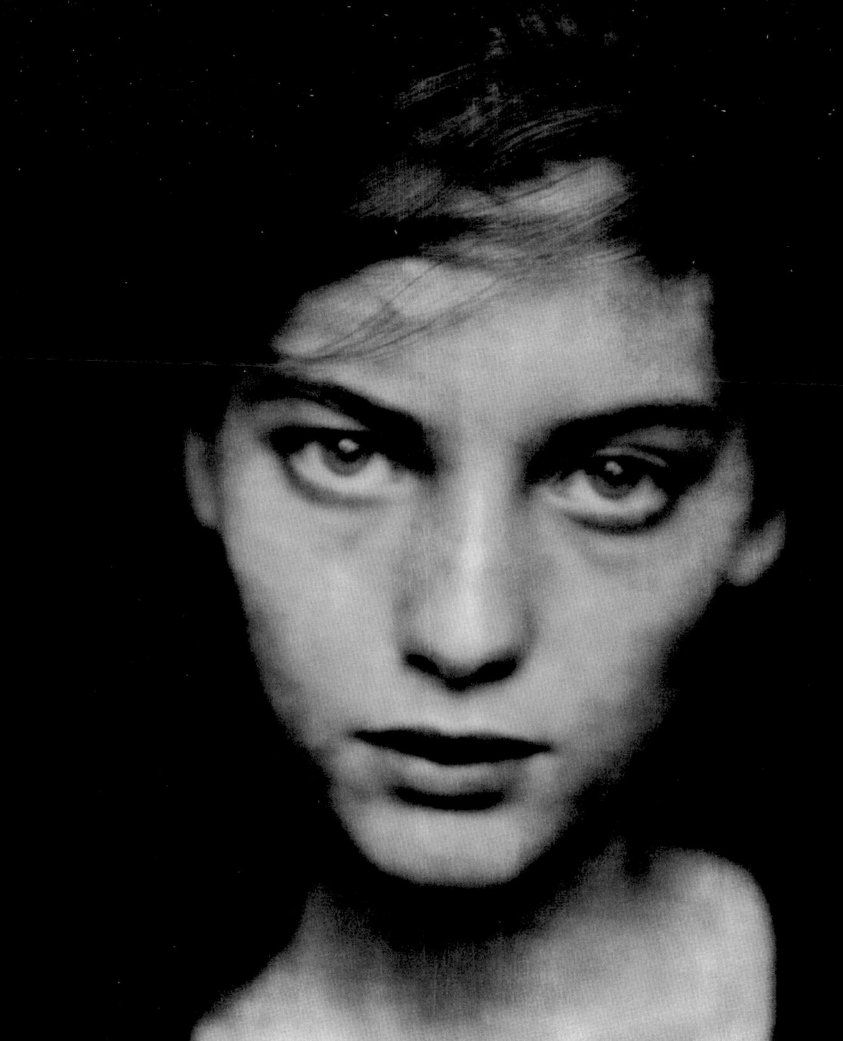

10. Ben, Paris, 2004.

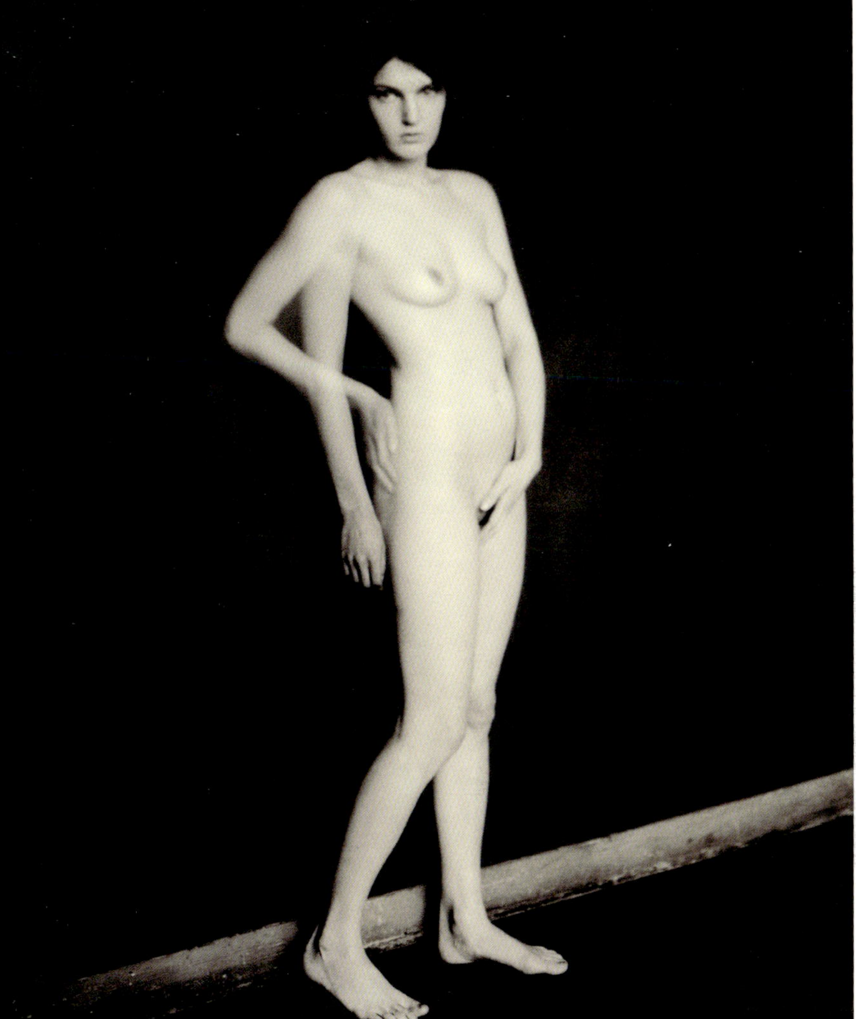

11. Jérôme, Paris, 2005.

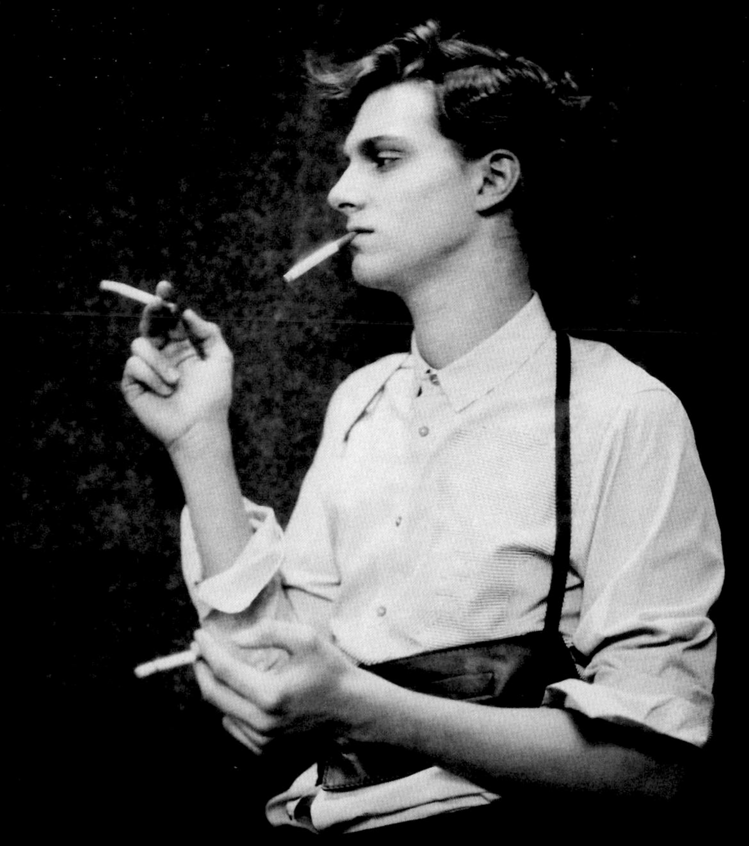

12. Guinevere, Paris, 1996.

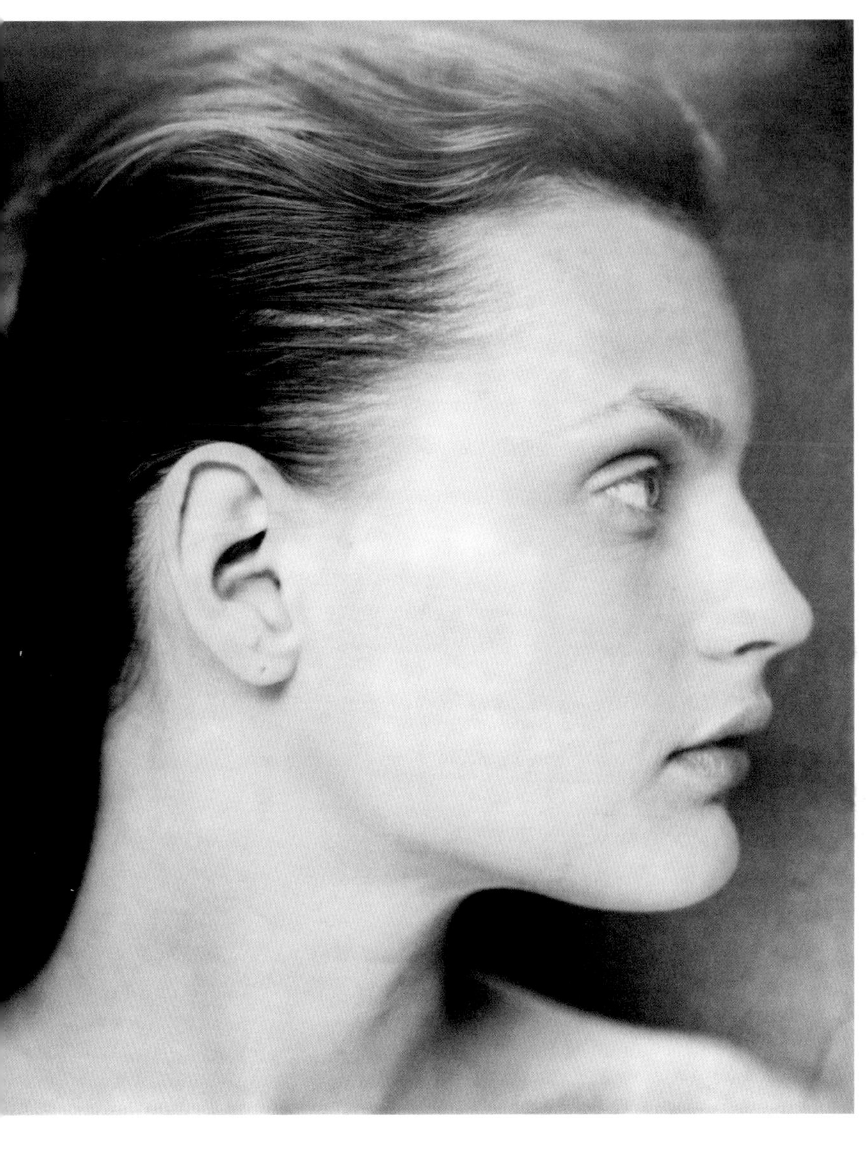

13. Sara, Paris, 2004.

Overleaf:
14. Theatre, Paris, 1998.

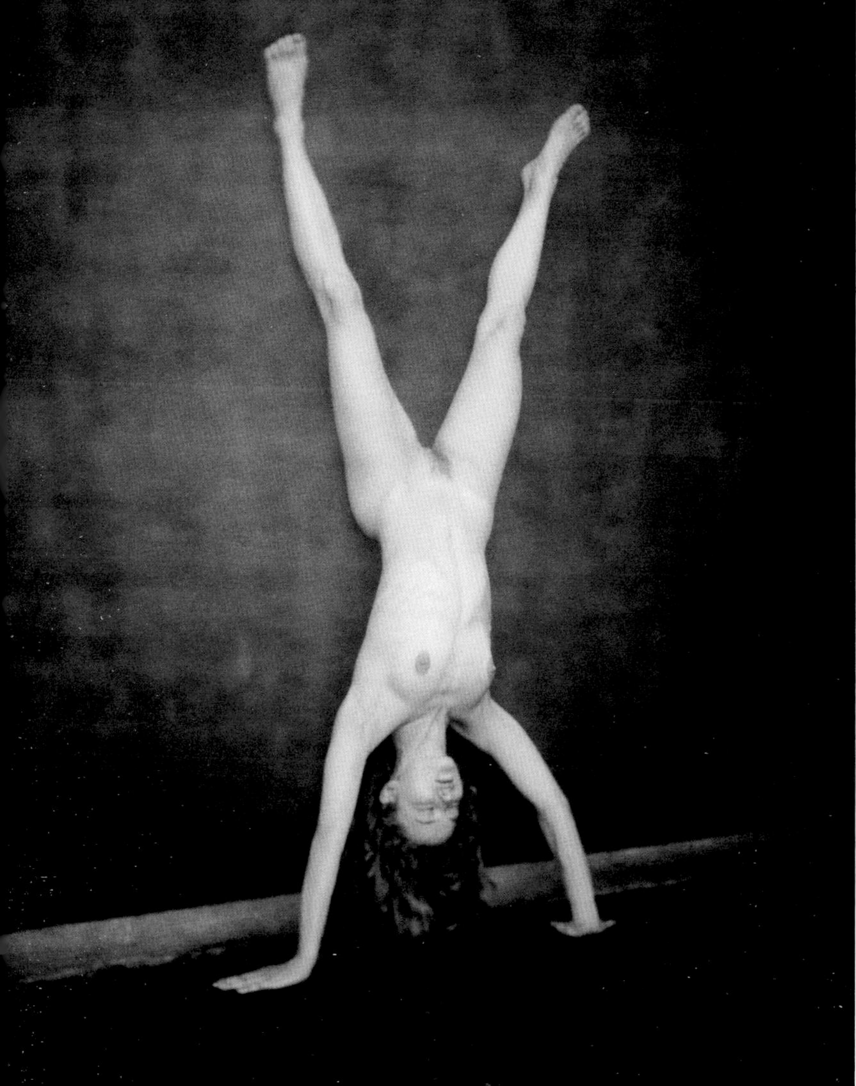

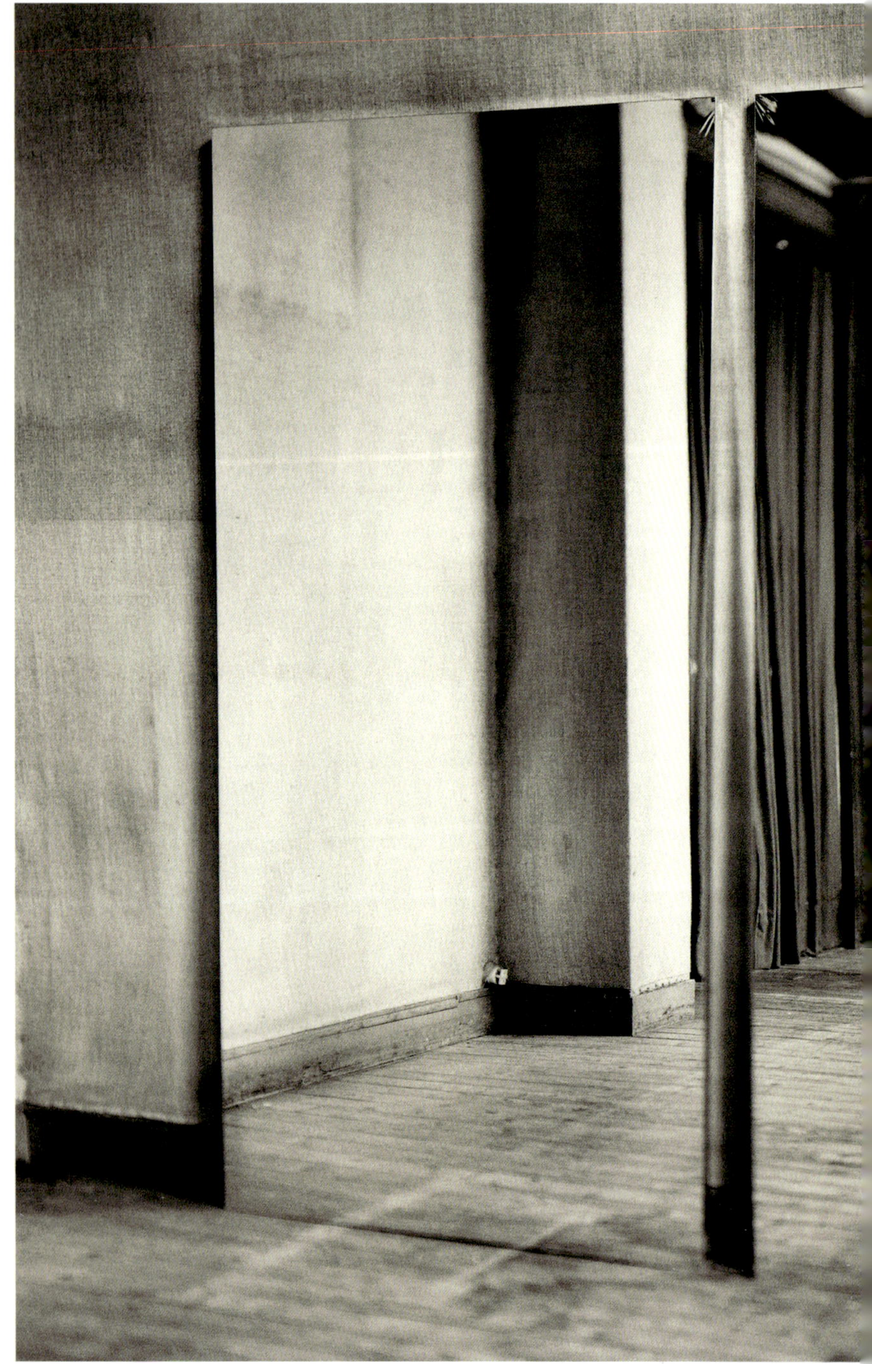

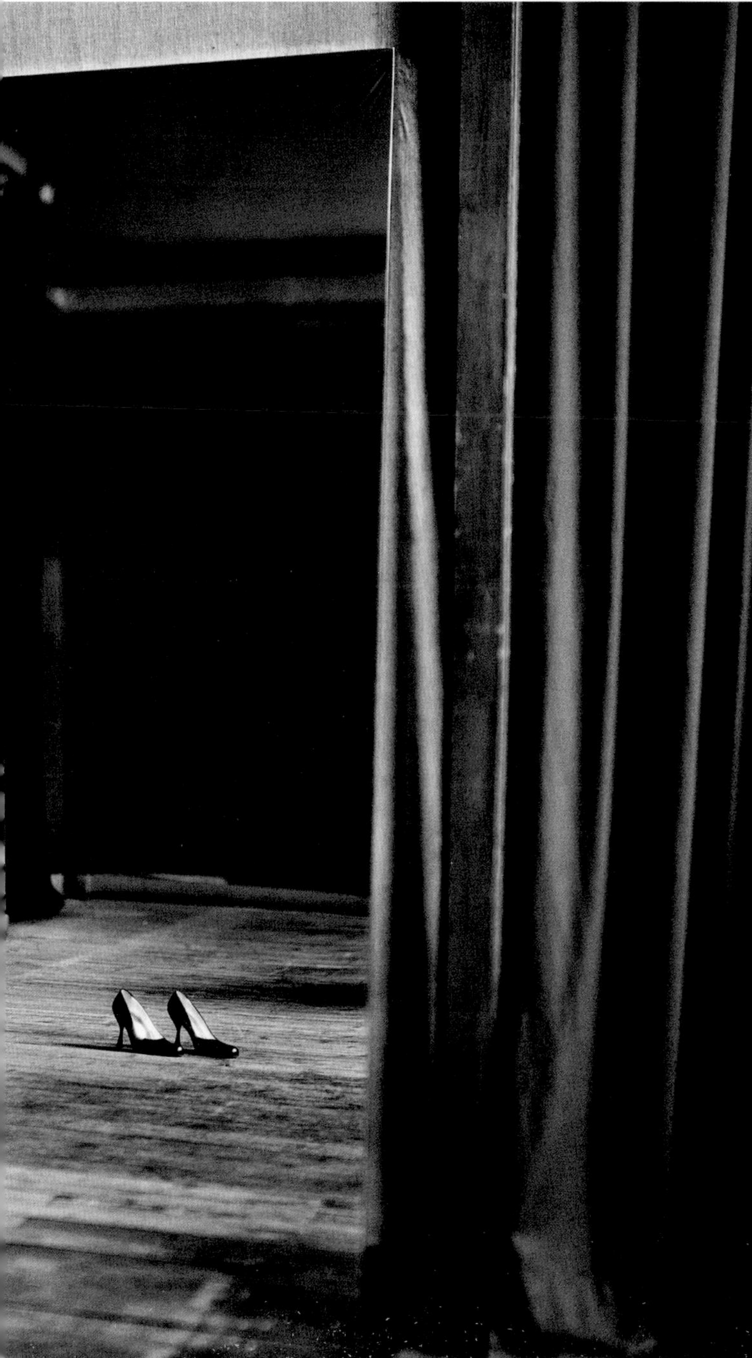

15. Self-portrait, Paris, 2010.

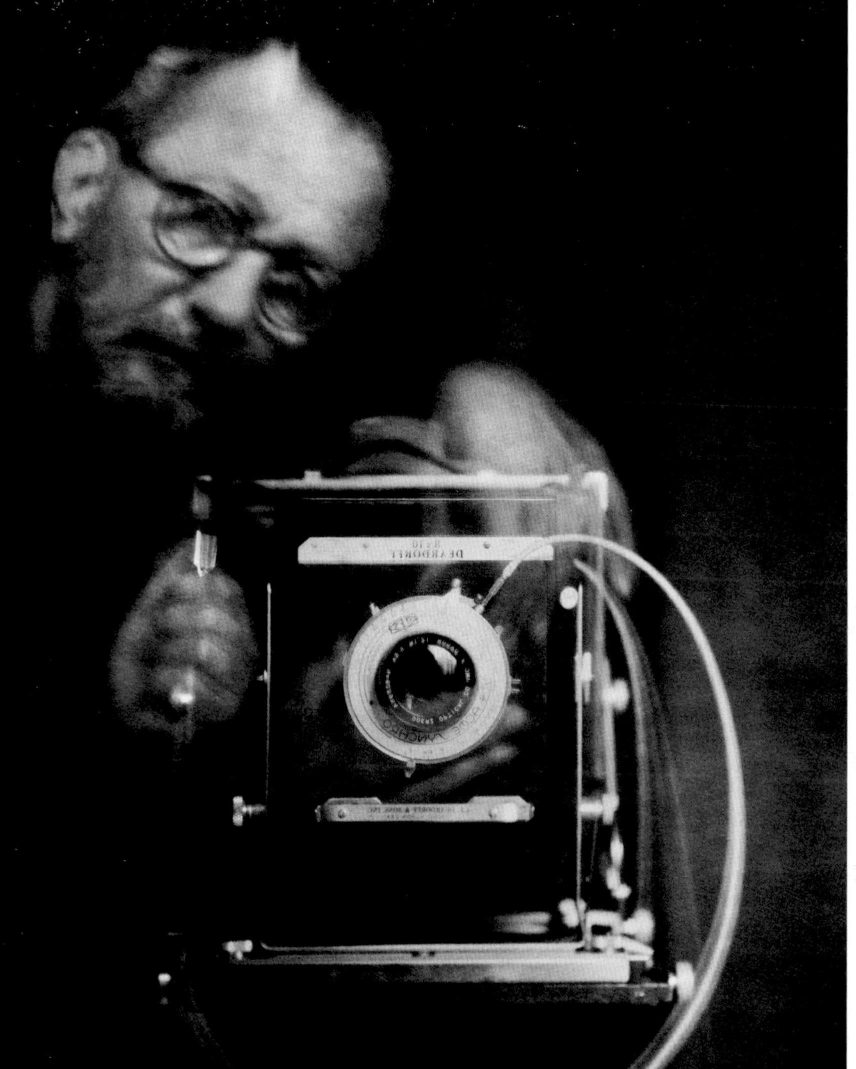

16. Light, Paris, 2002.

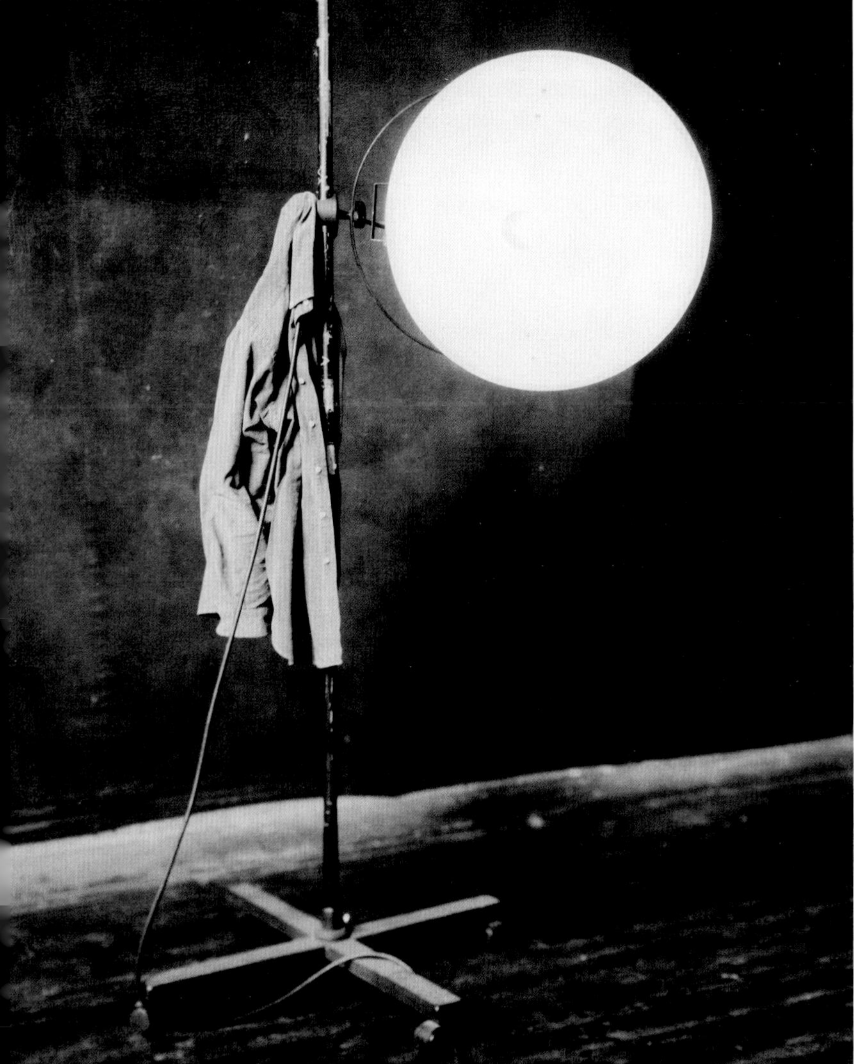

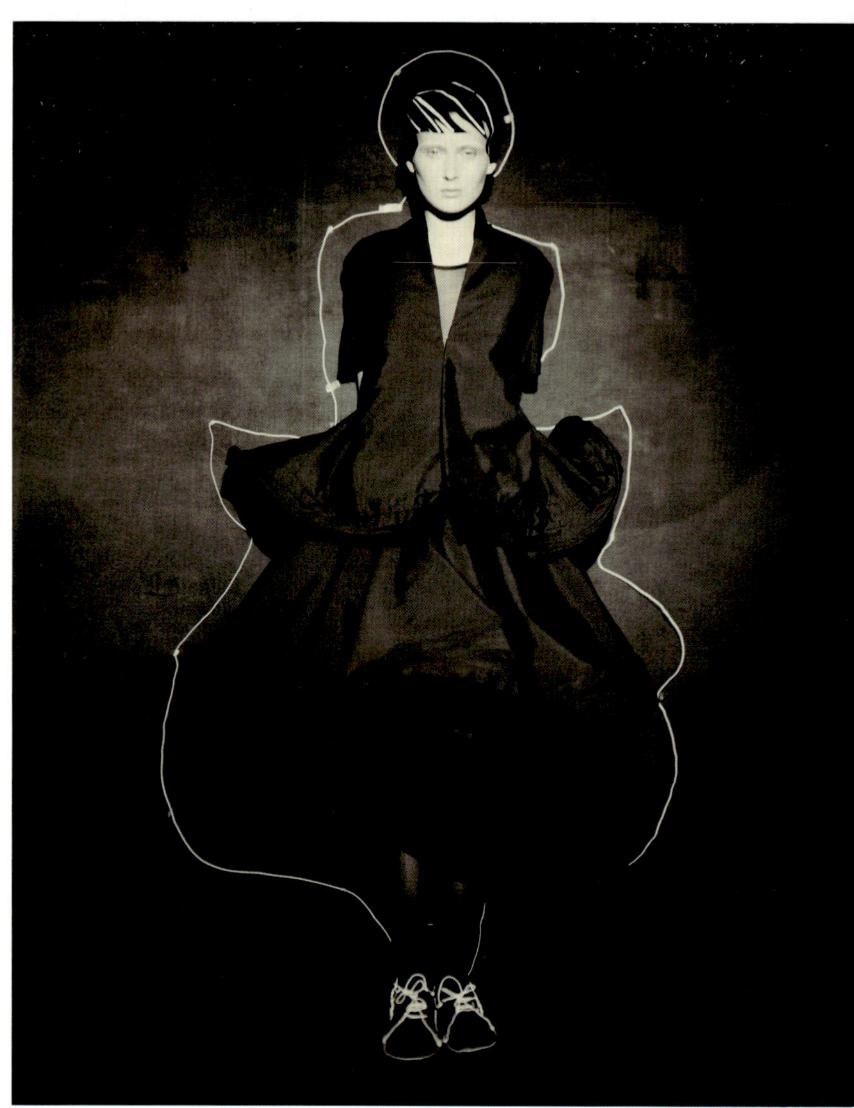

17 & 18. Audrey, Paris, 1998.

Overleaf:
19. Studio, Paris, 2002.

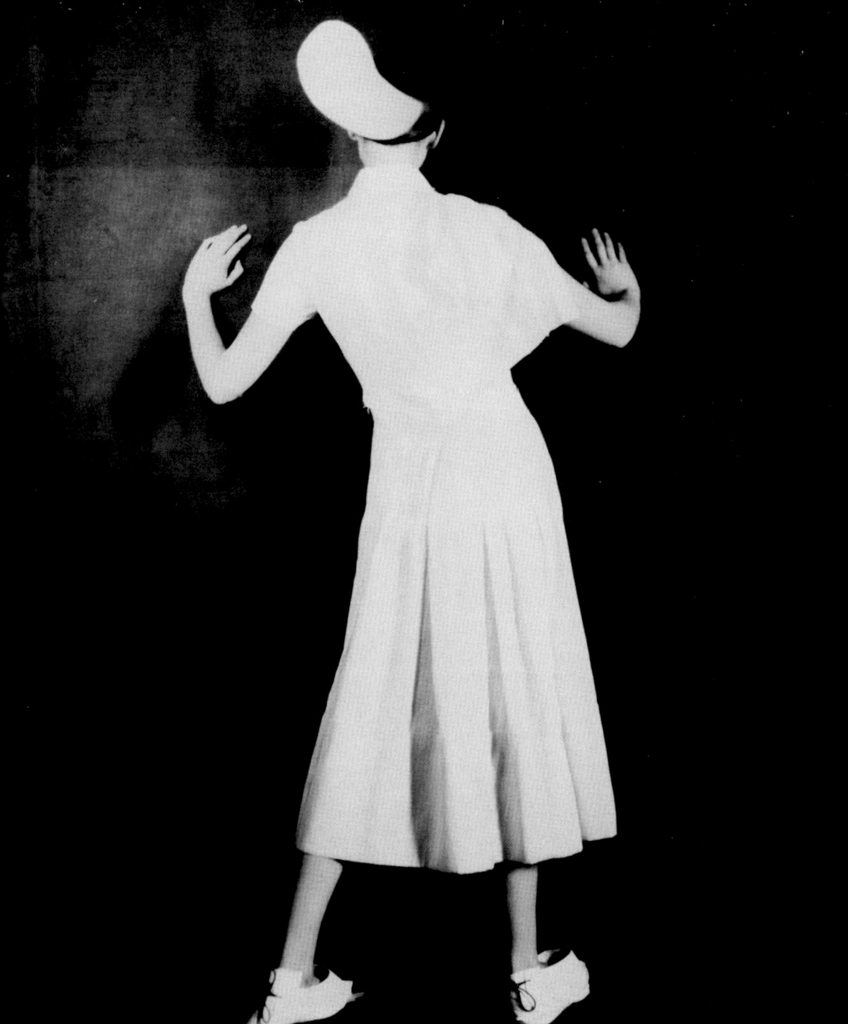

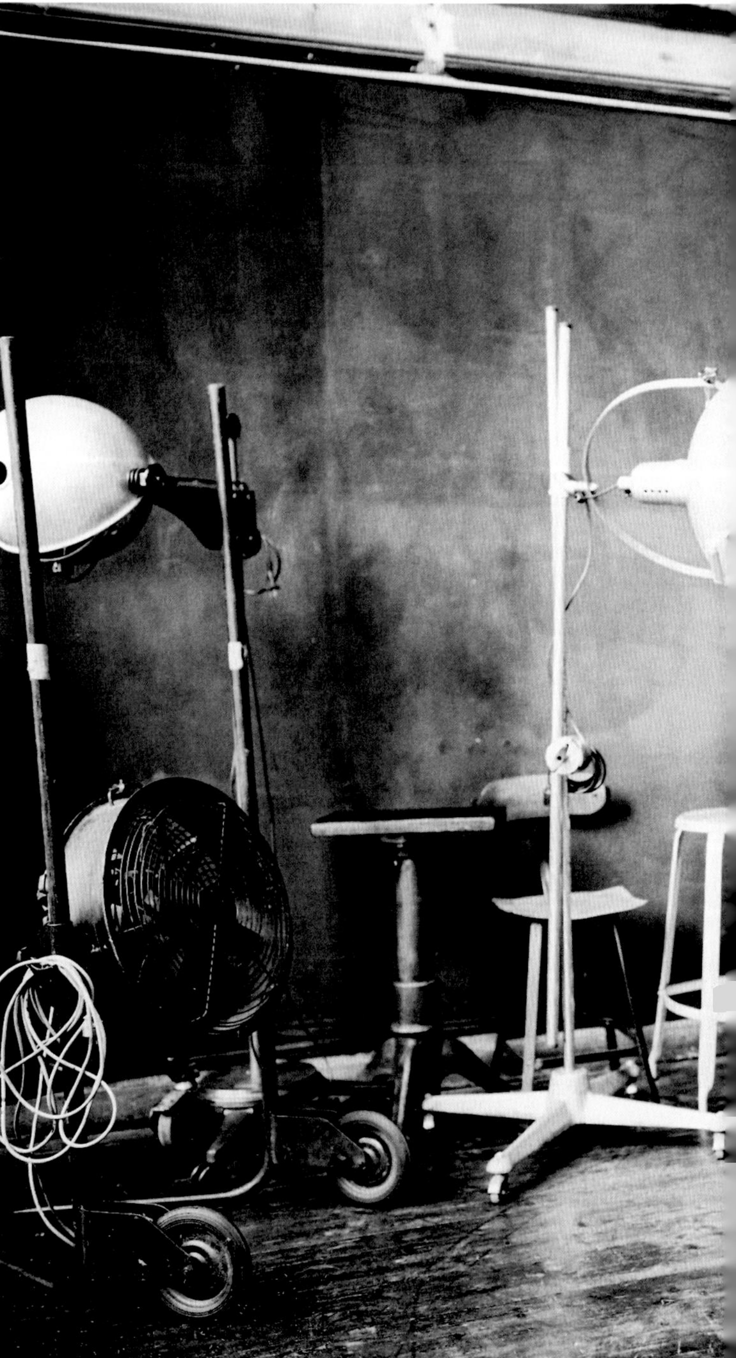

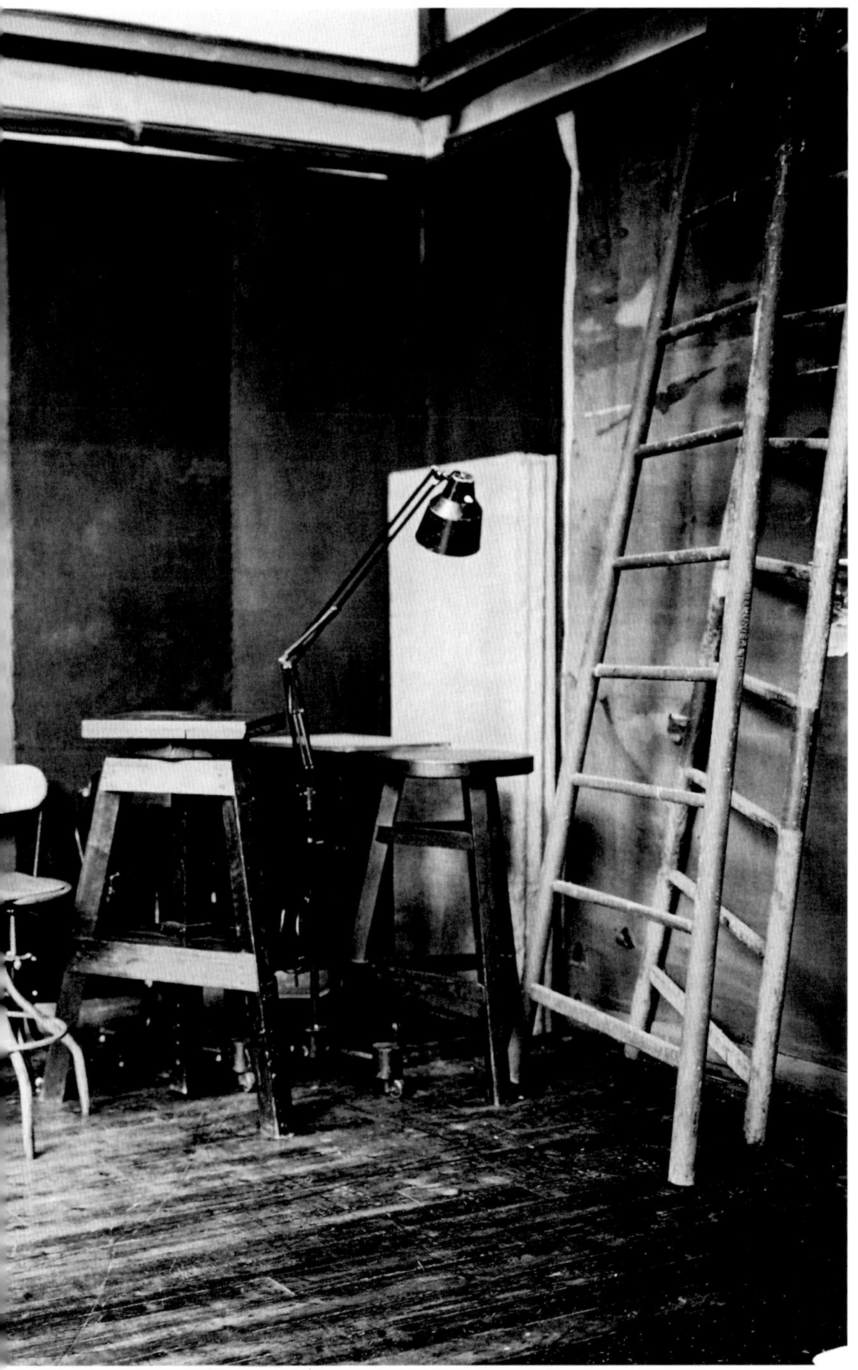

20. Jeenu, Paris, 2018.

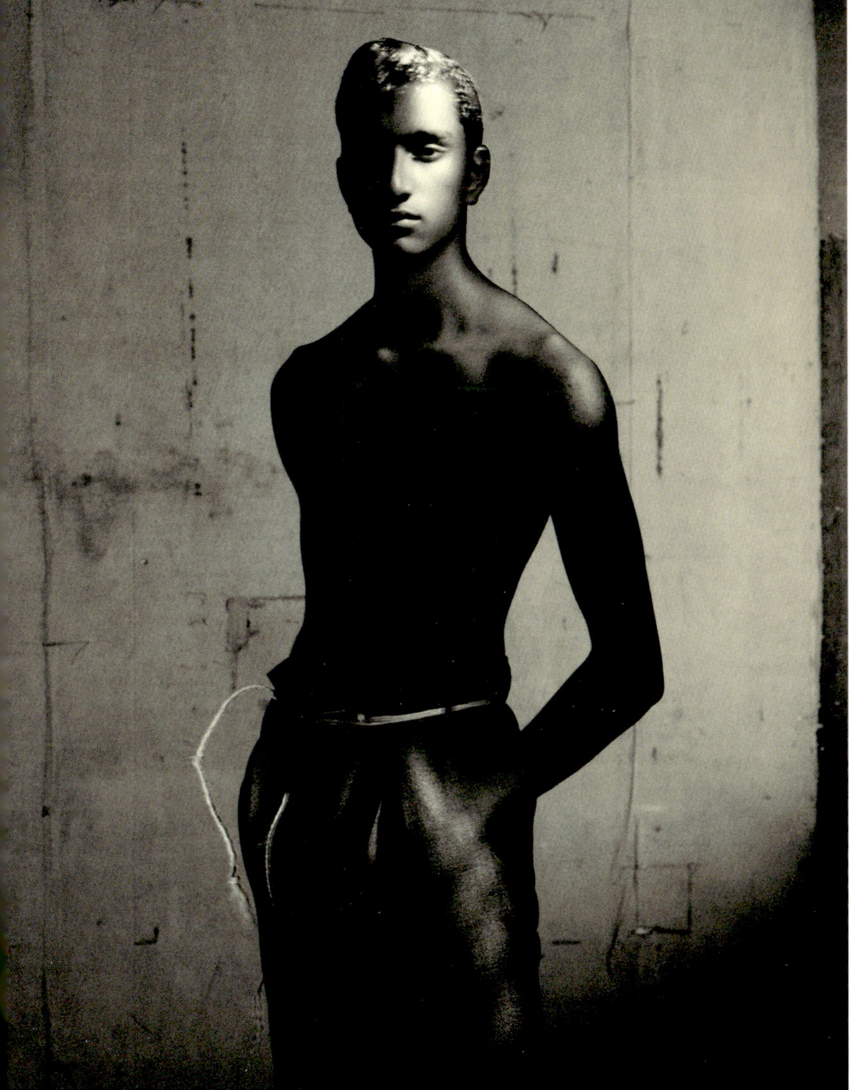

21. Naomi, Paris, 1996.

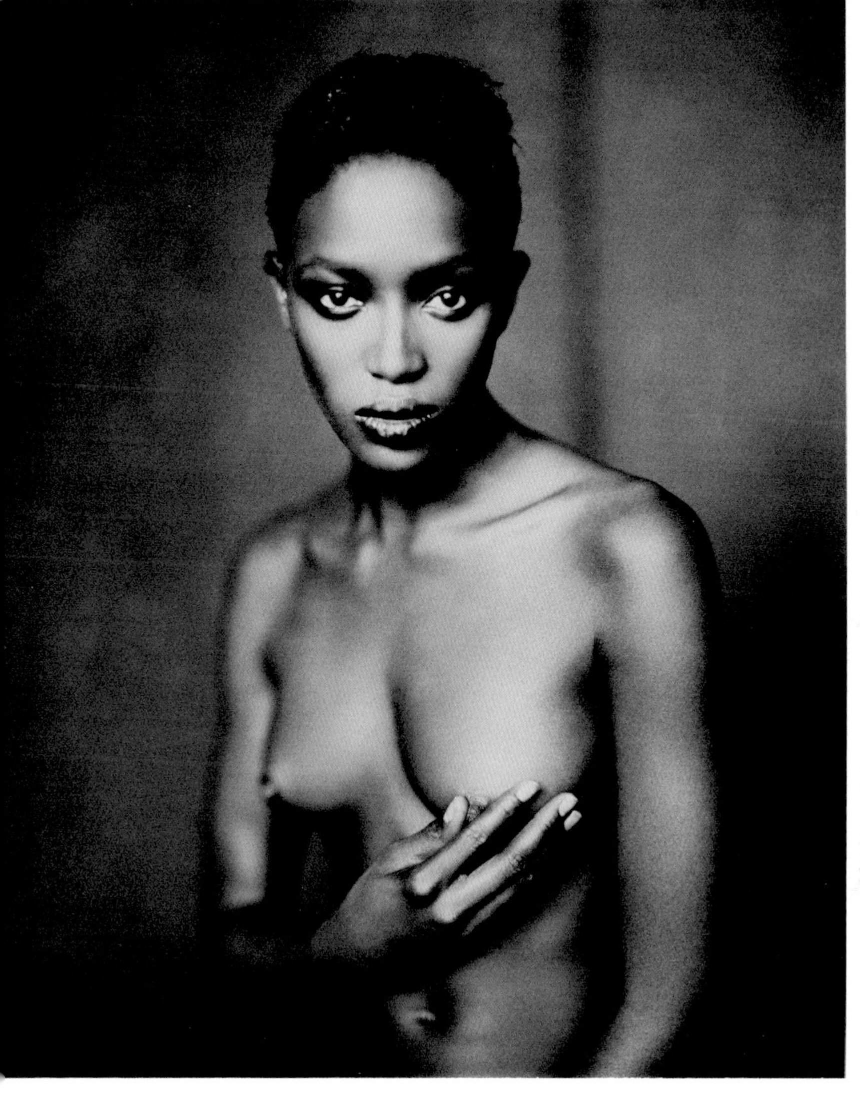

22. Film holder, Paris, 2004.

Overleaf:
23. Ravenna, Paris, 2003.

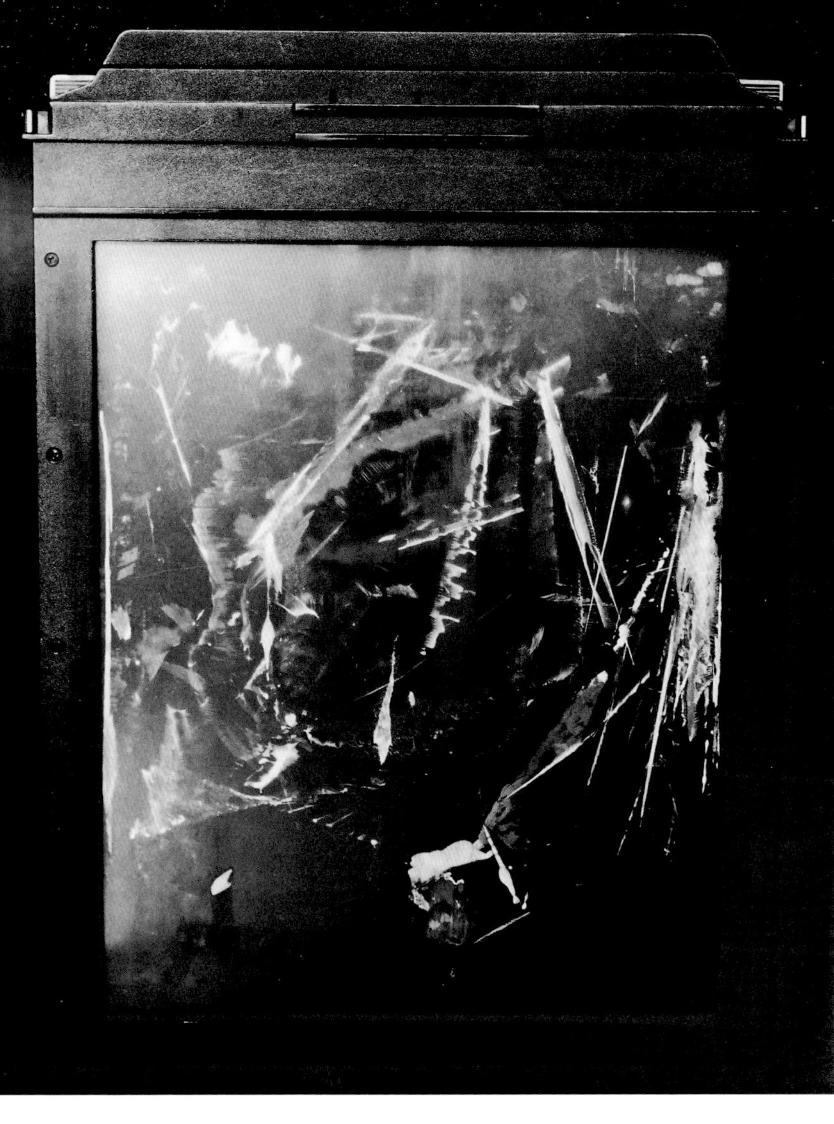

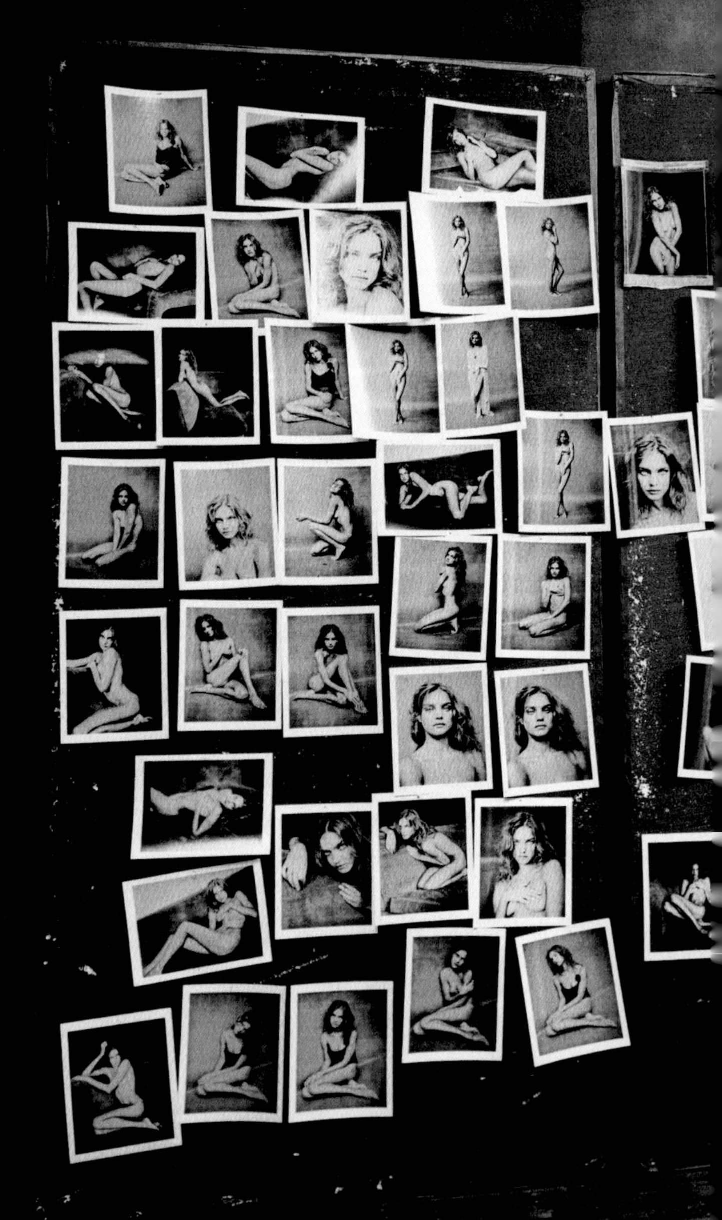

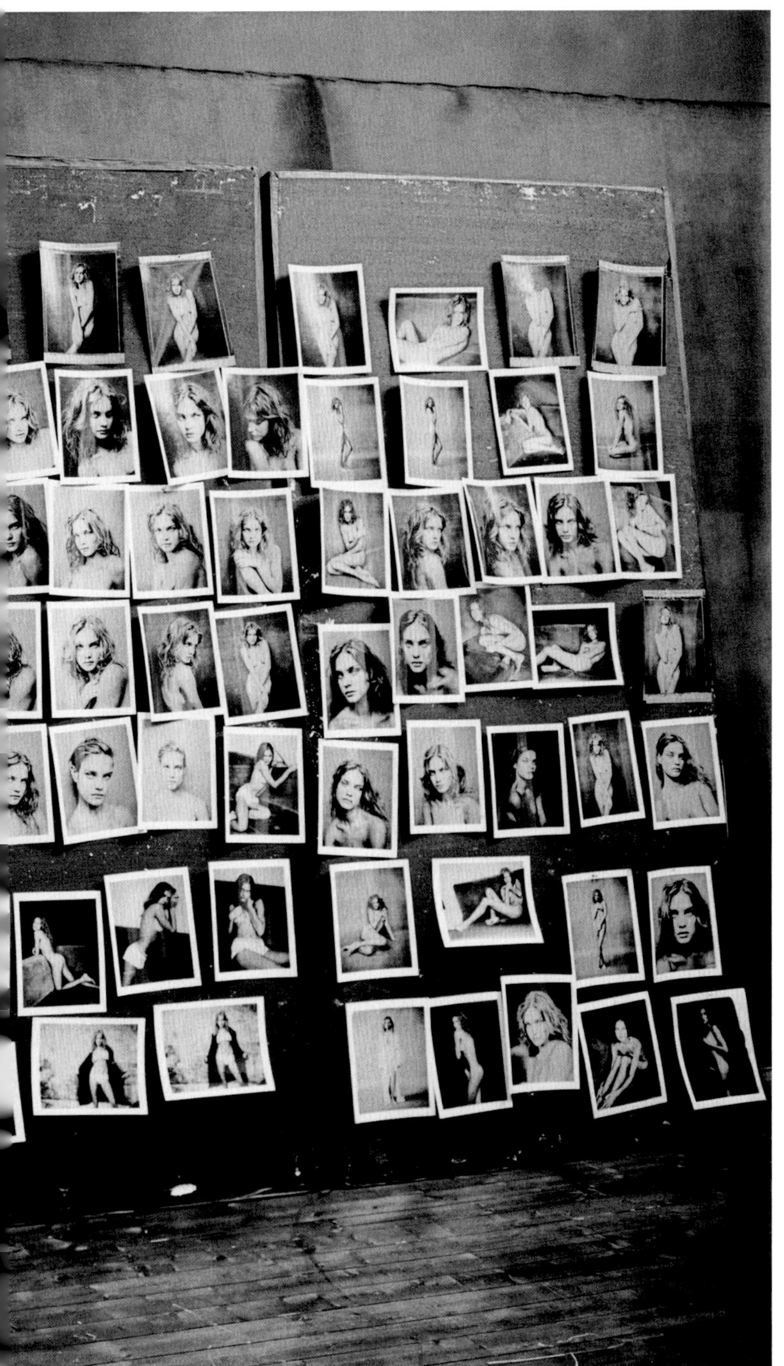

24. Sara, Paris, 2004.

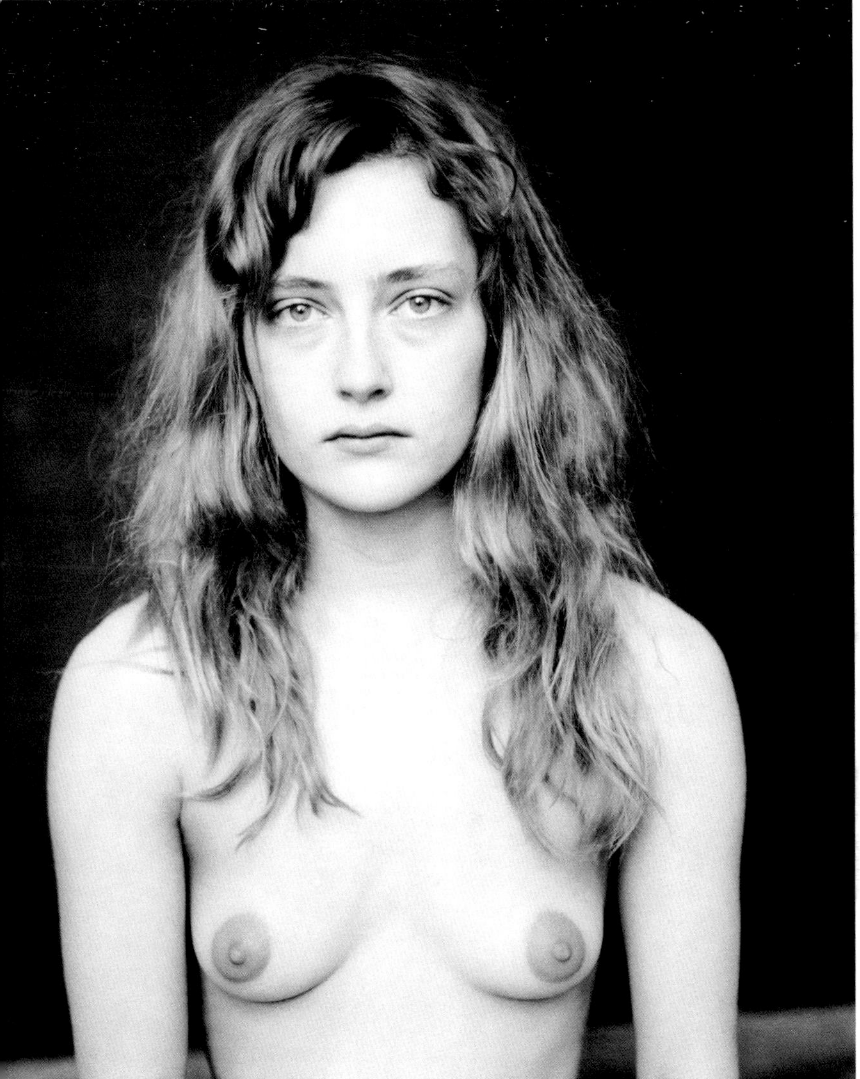

25. Billy, Paris, 1998.

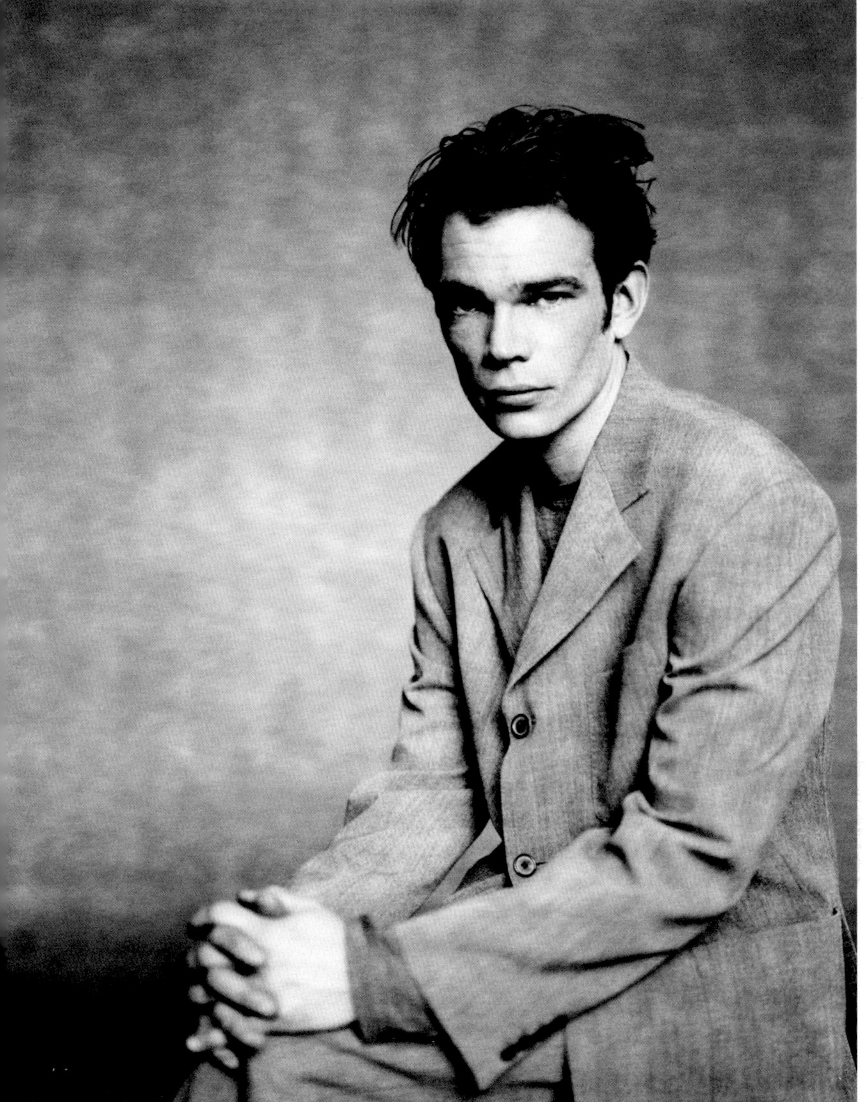

26. Guinevere, Paris, 2004.

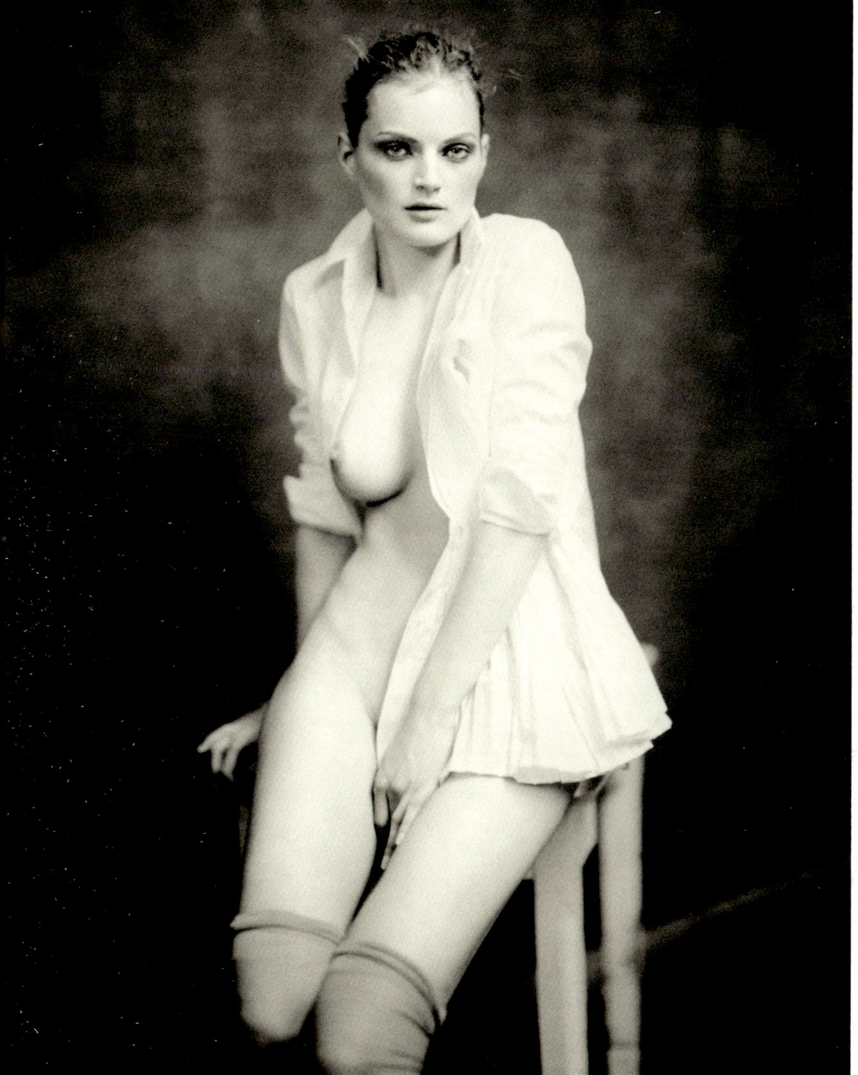

27. John Galliano, Paris, 2006.

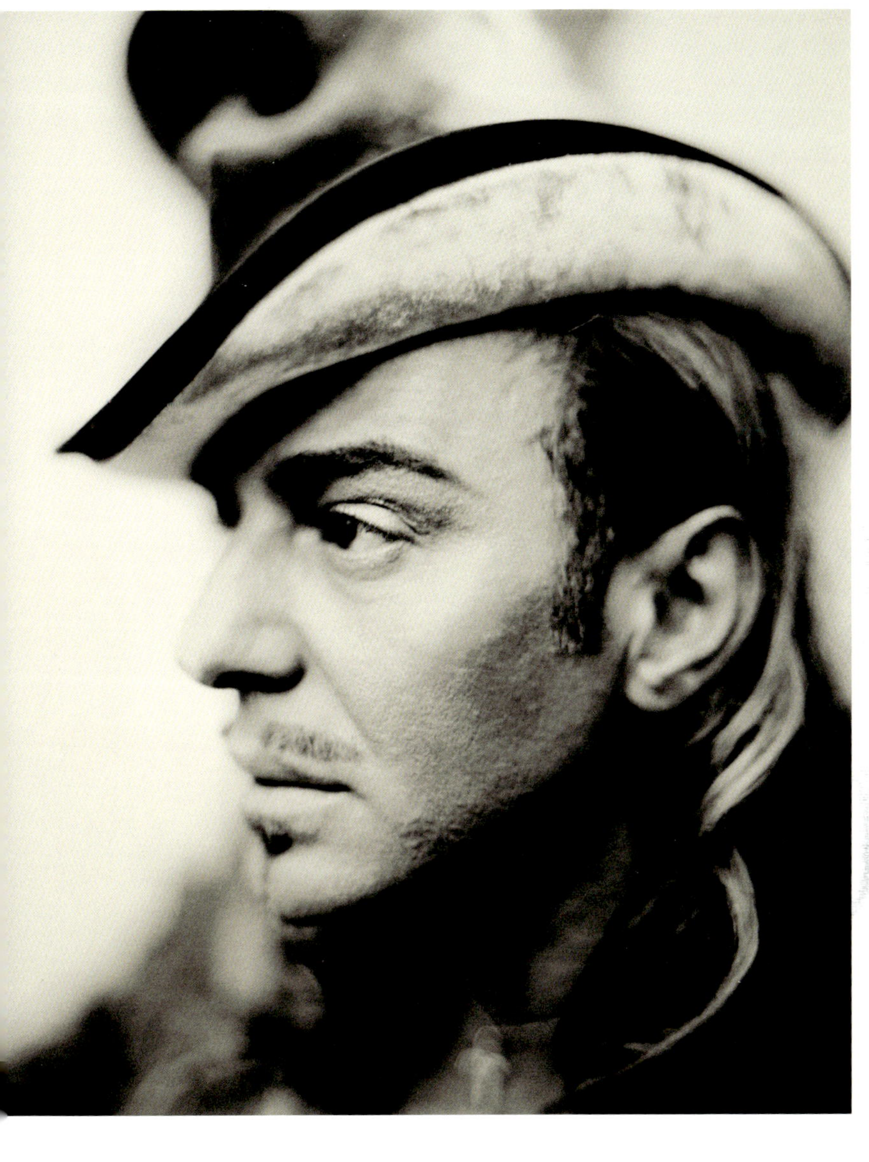

28. Saskia, Paris, 2012.

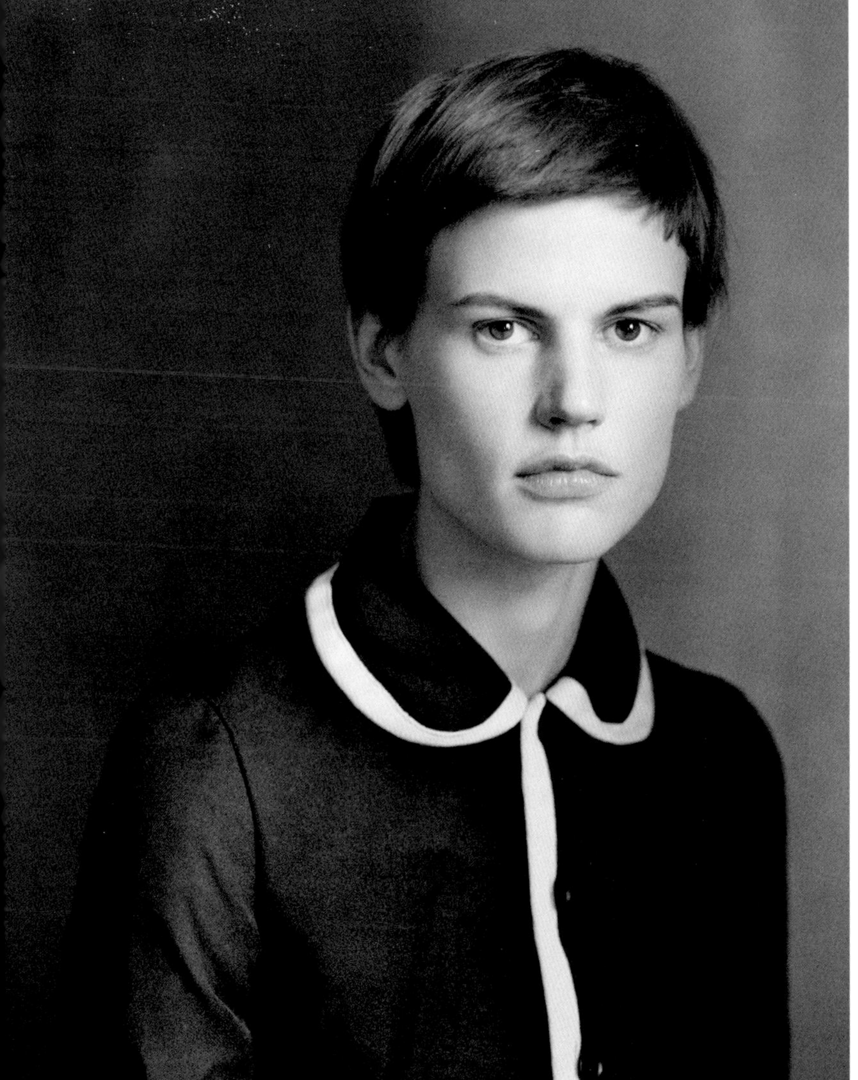

29. Guinevere, Paris, 1996.

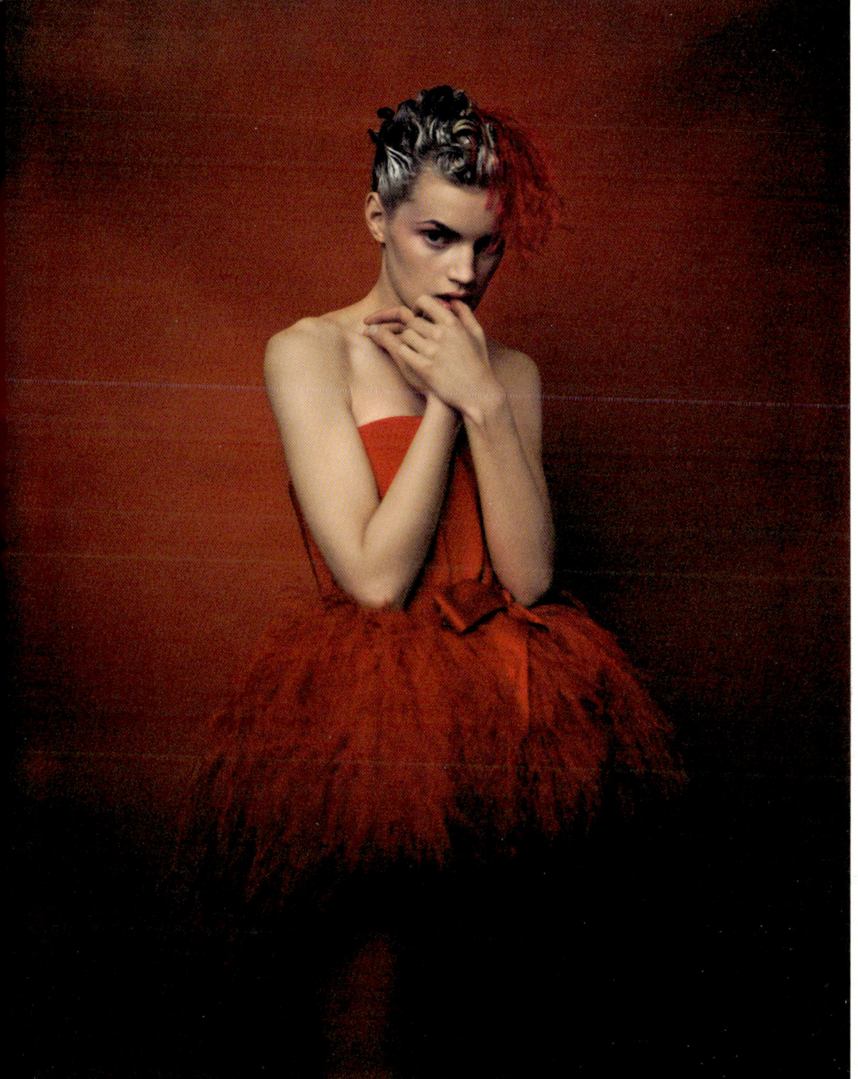

30. Guinevere with Guapi, Paris, 1996.

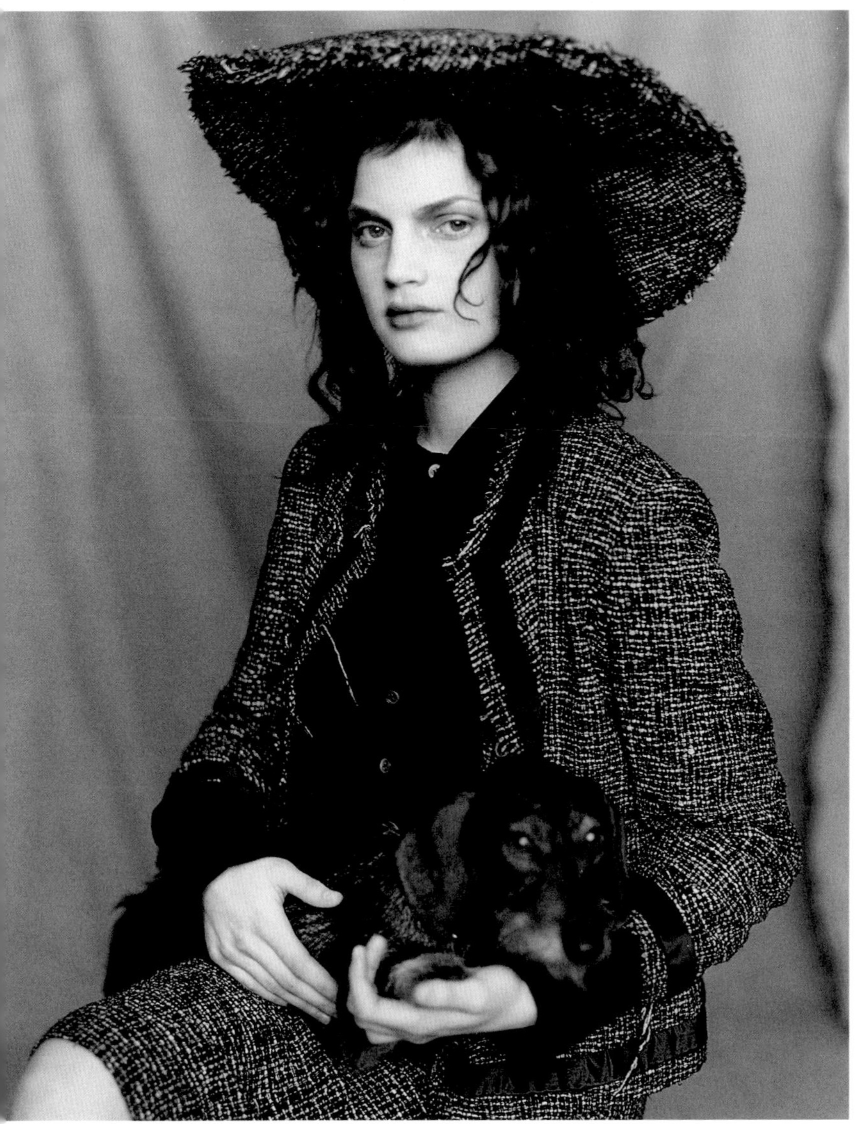

31. Stella, Verona, 2019.

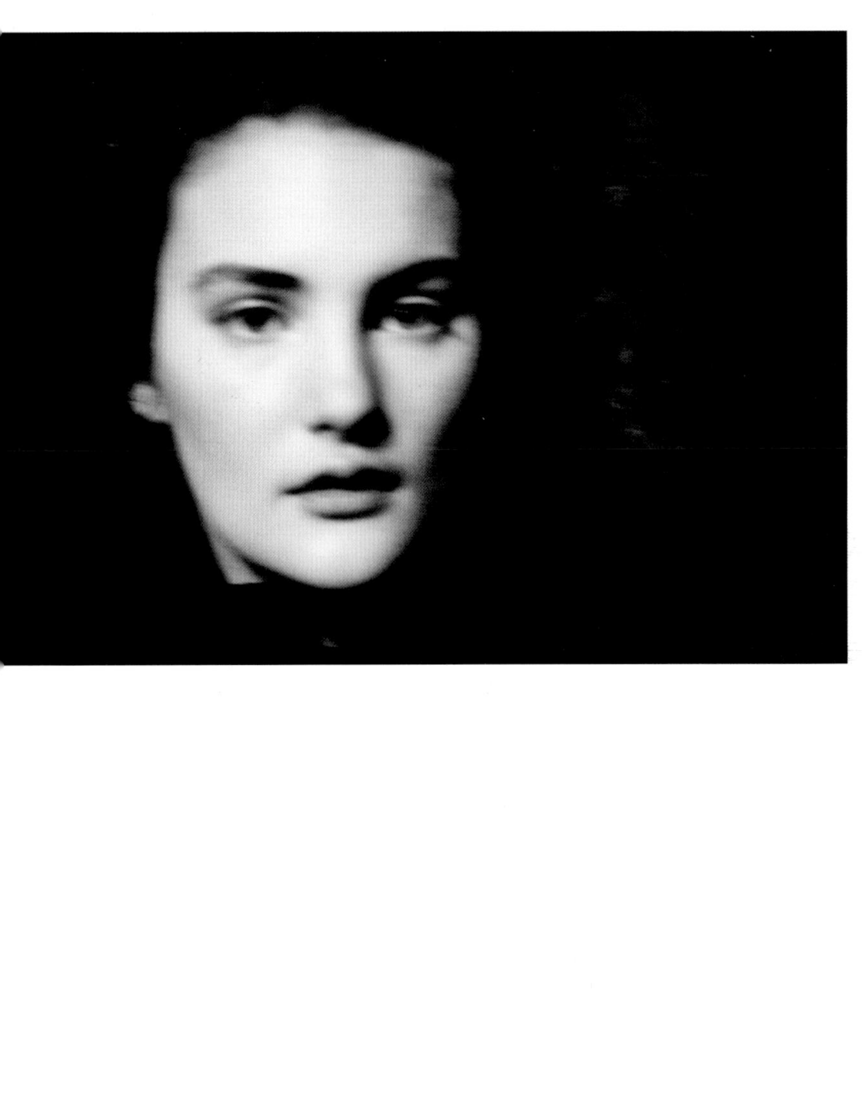

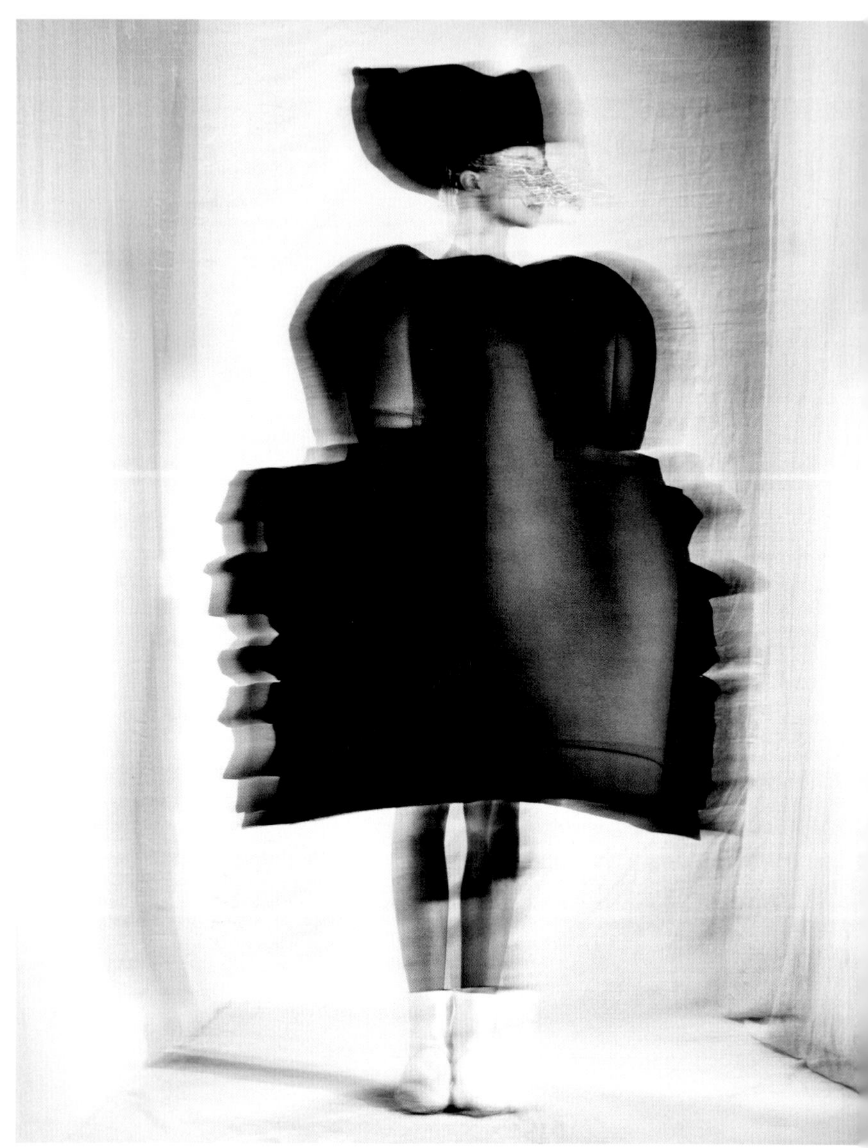

32. Anna, Tokyo, 2016.
33. Charles, Paris, 2005.

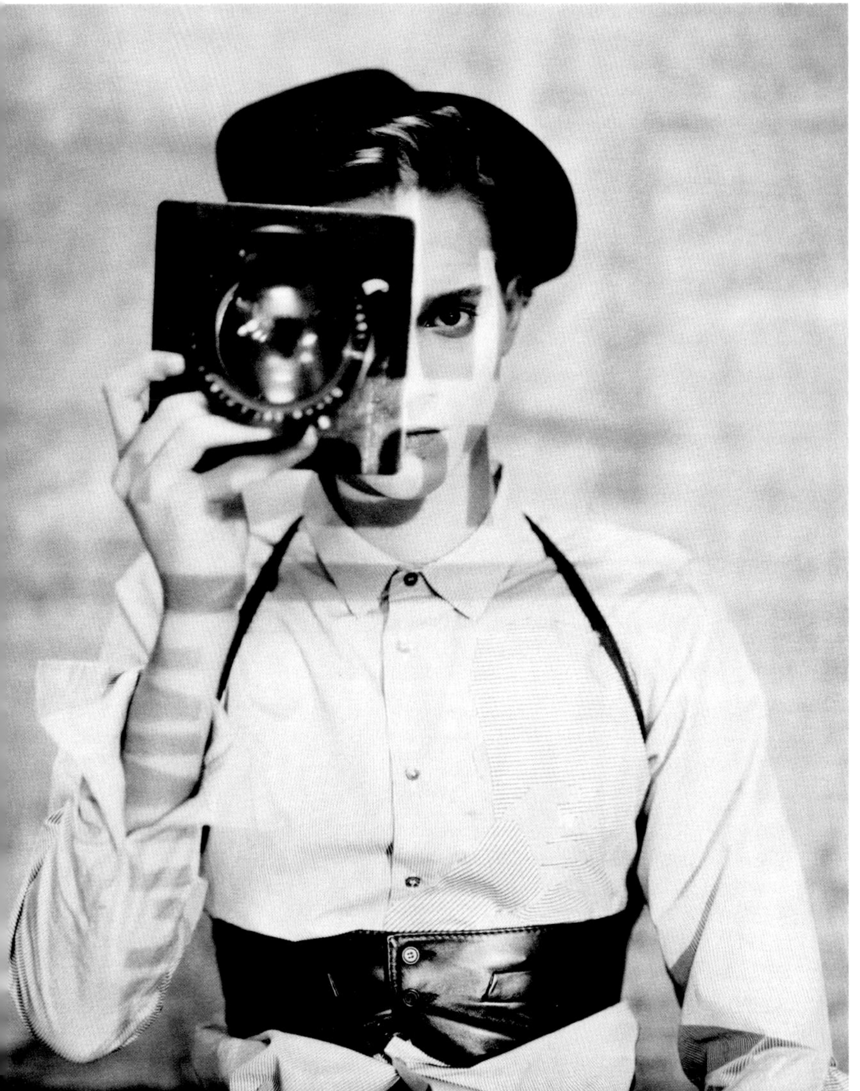

34. Studio, Paris, 2002.

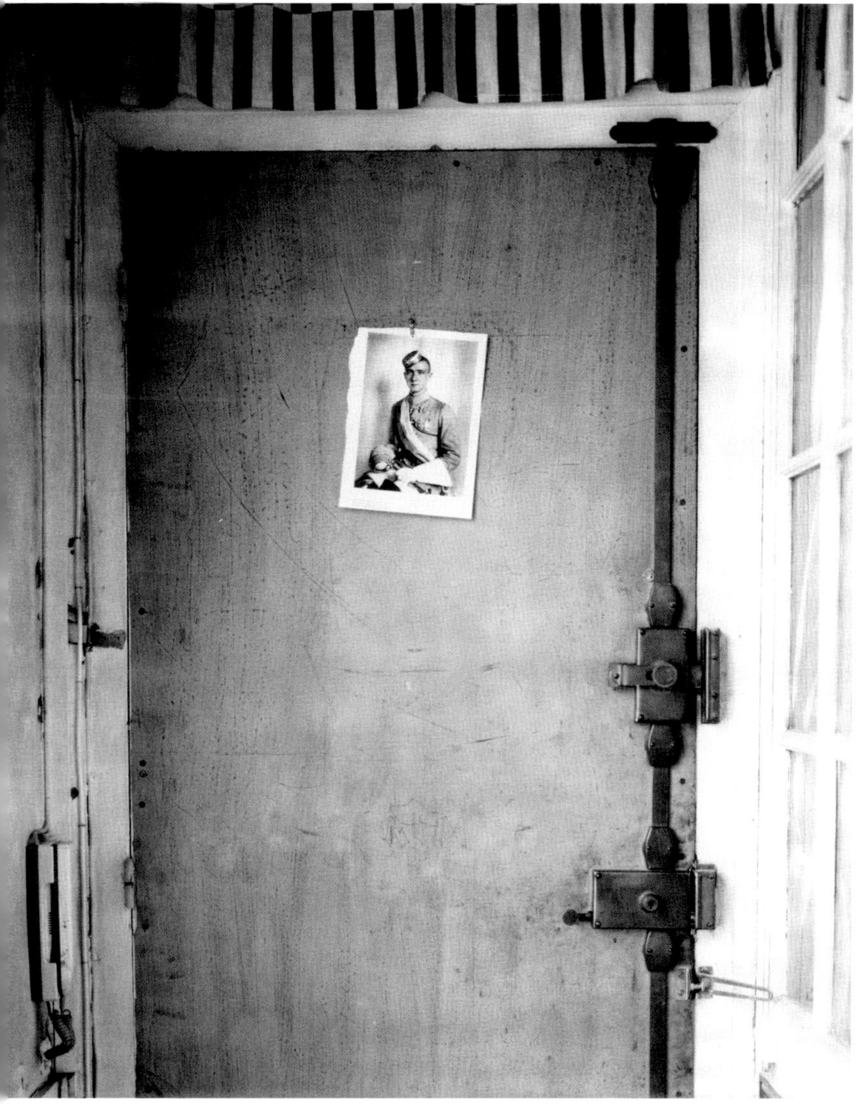

35. Lida & Alexandra, Paris, 1998.

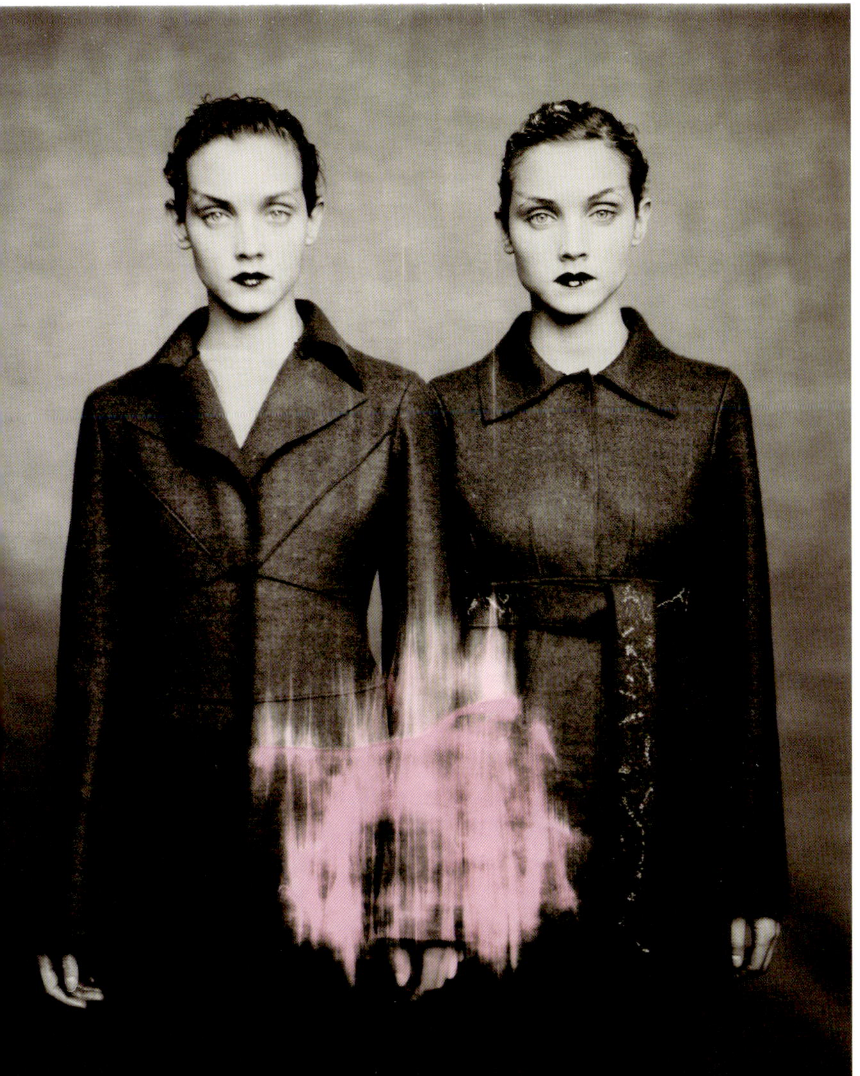

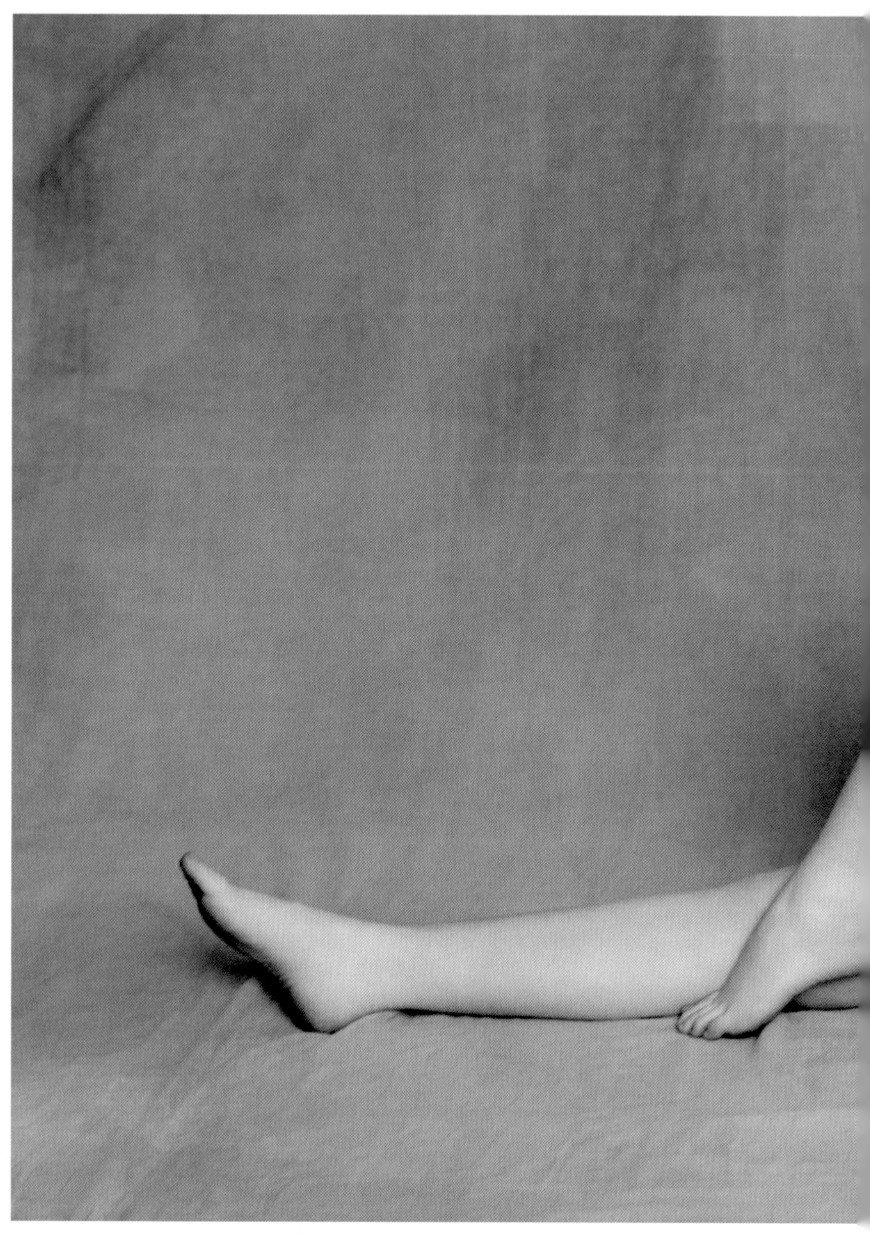

36. Tess, Paris, 2019.

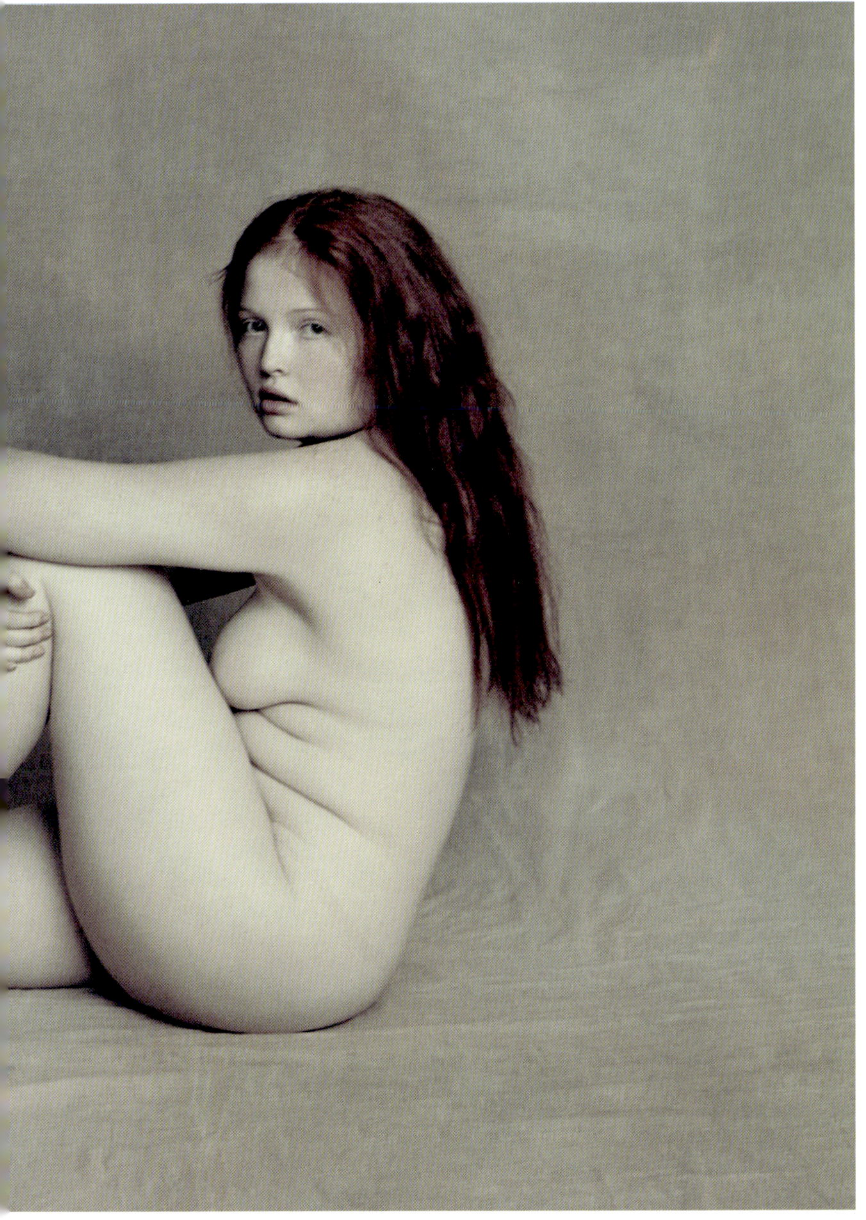

37. Guinevere, Paris, 2004.

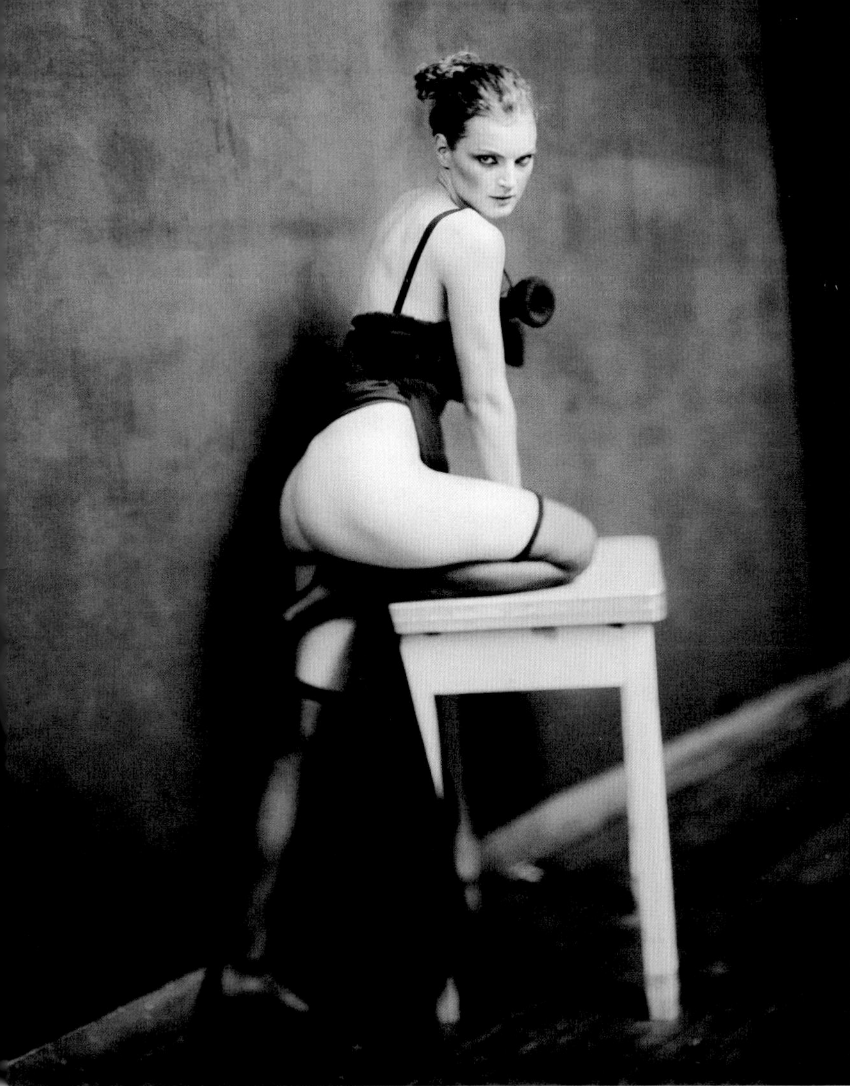

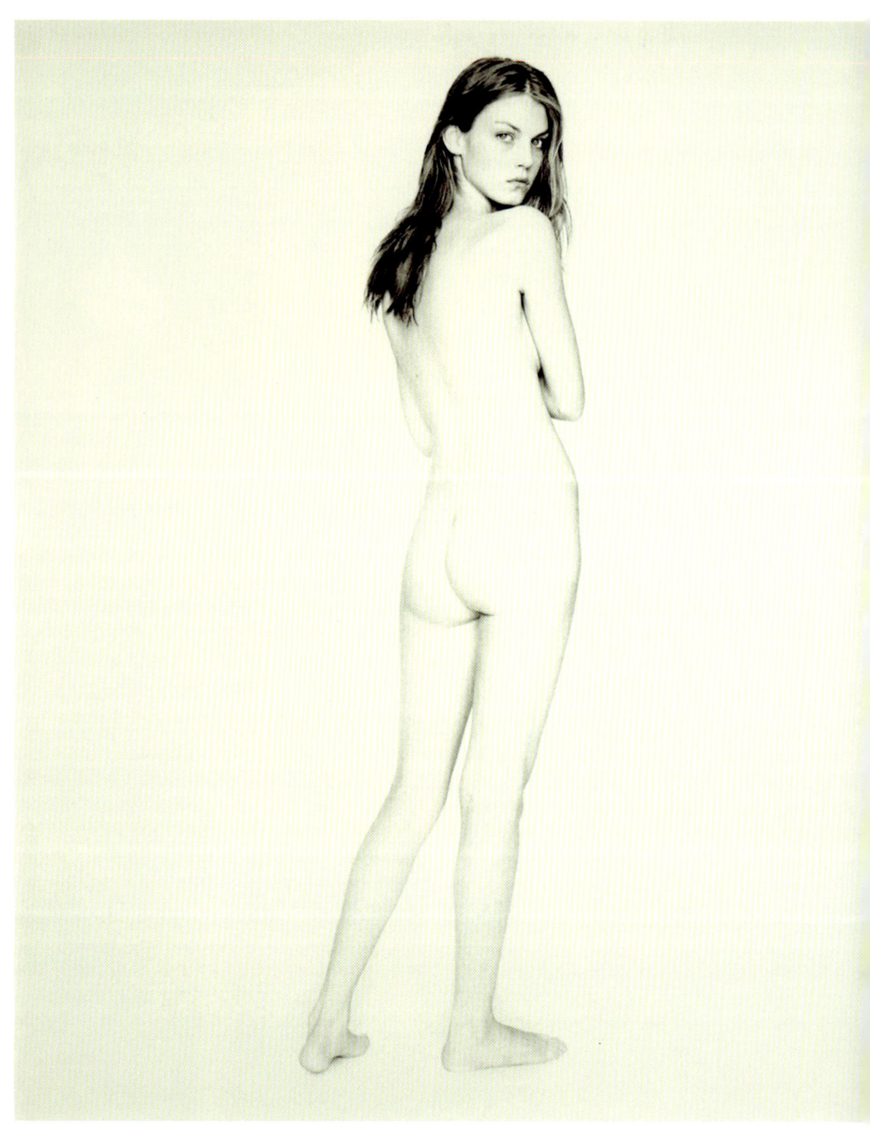

38. Angela, Paris, 1998.
39. Meg, Paris, 1986.

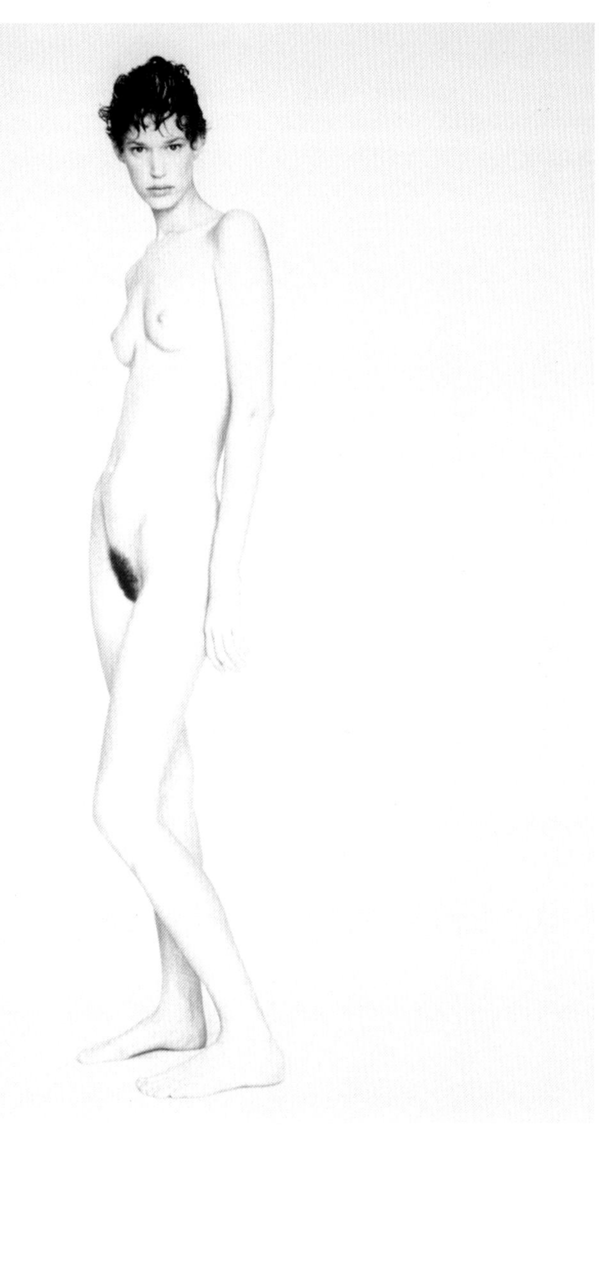

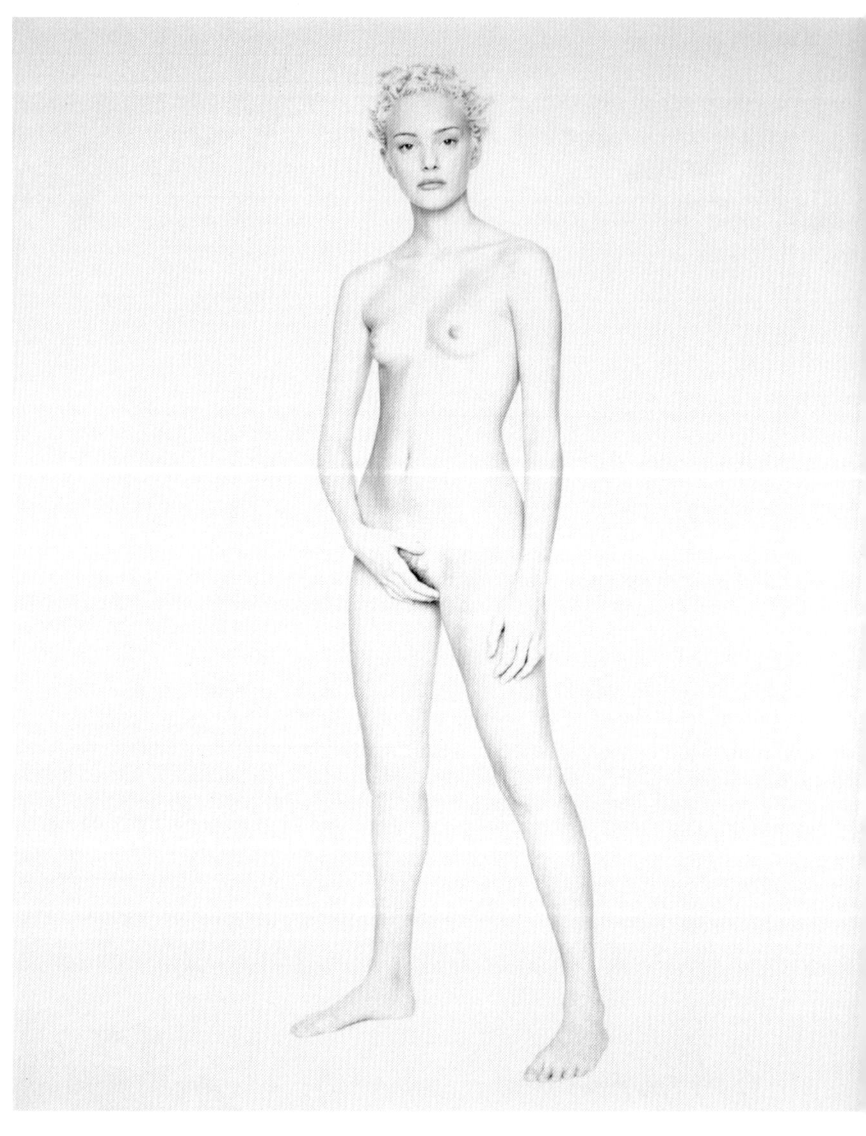

40. Jaime, Paris, 1993.
41. Milla, Paris, 1998.

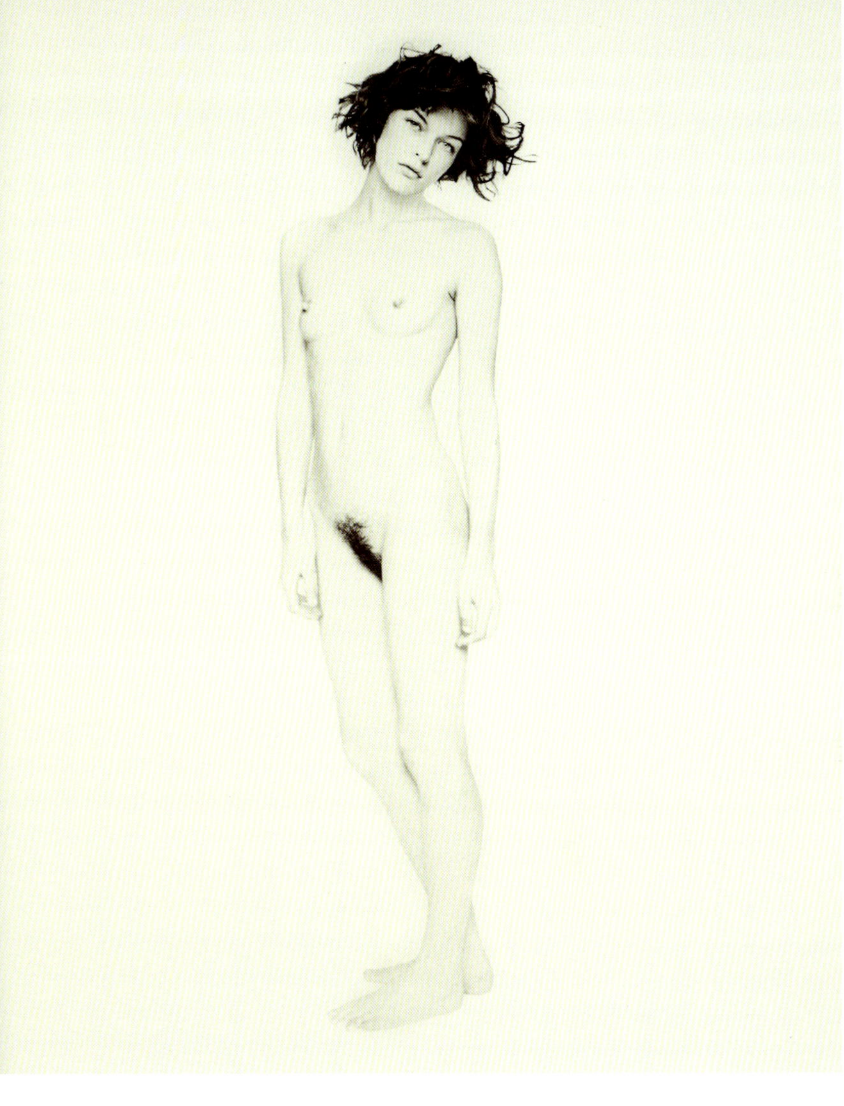

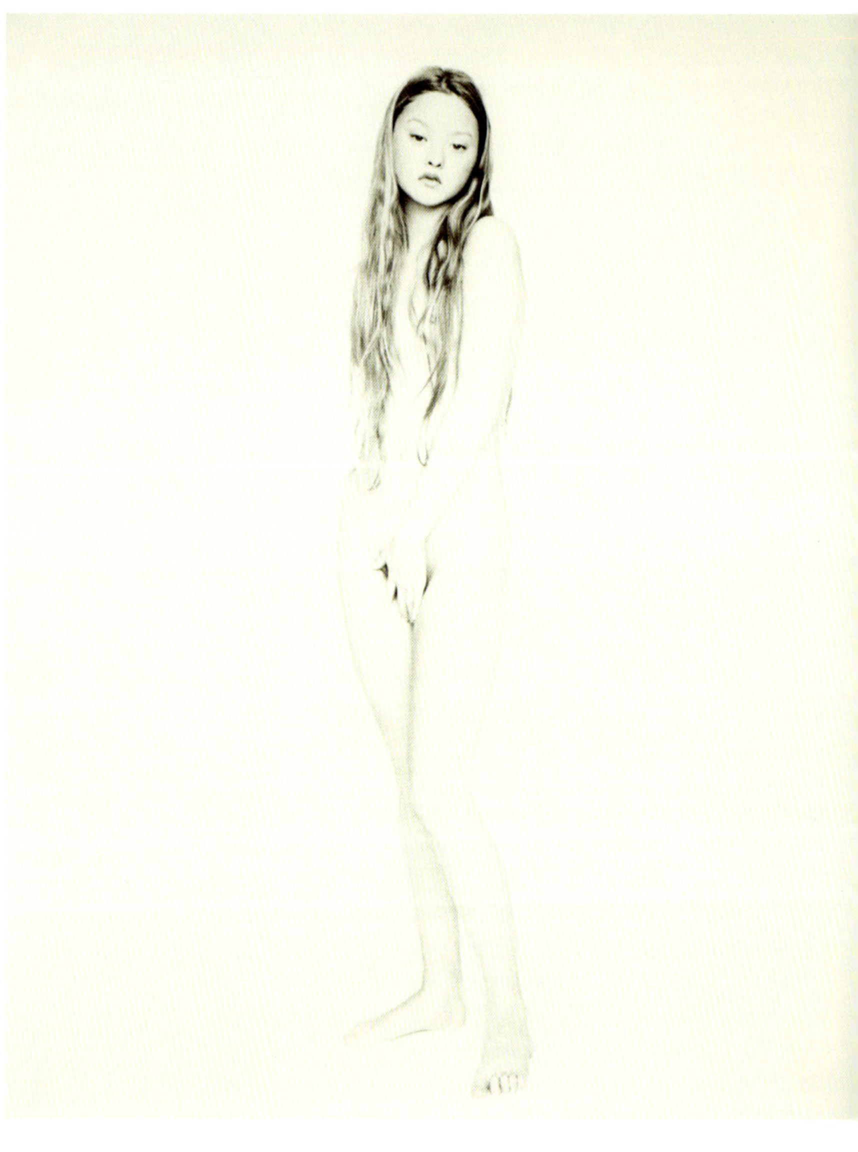

42. Devon, Paris, 1999.
43. Guinevere, Paris, 1995.

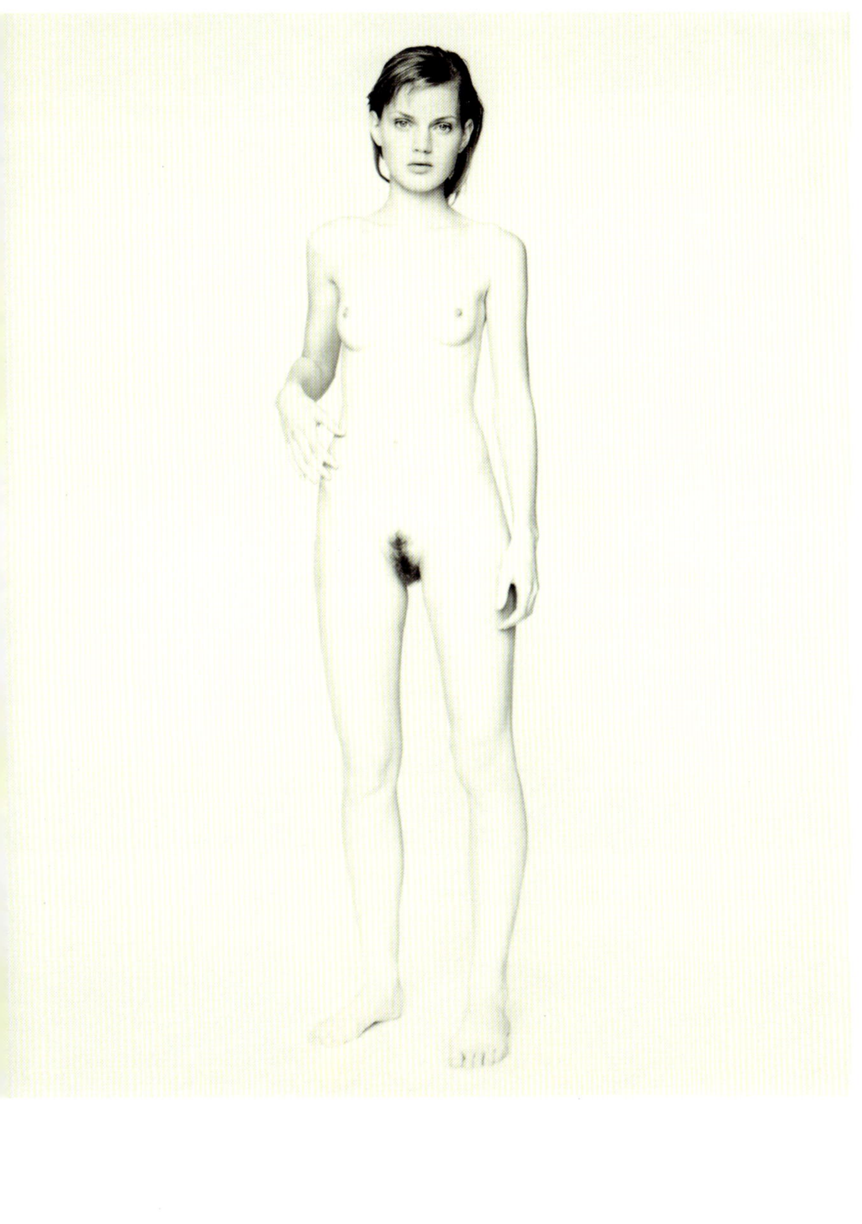

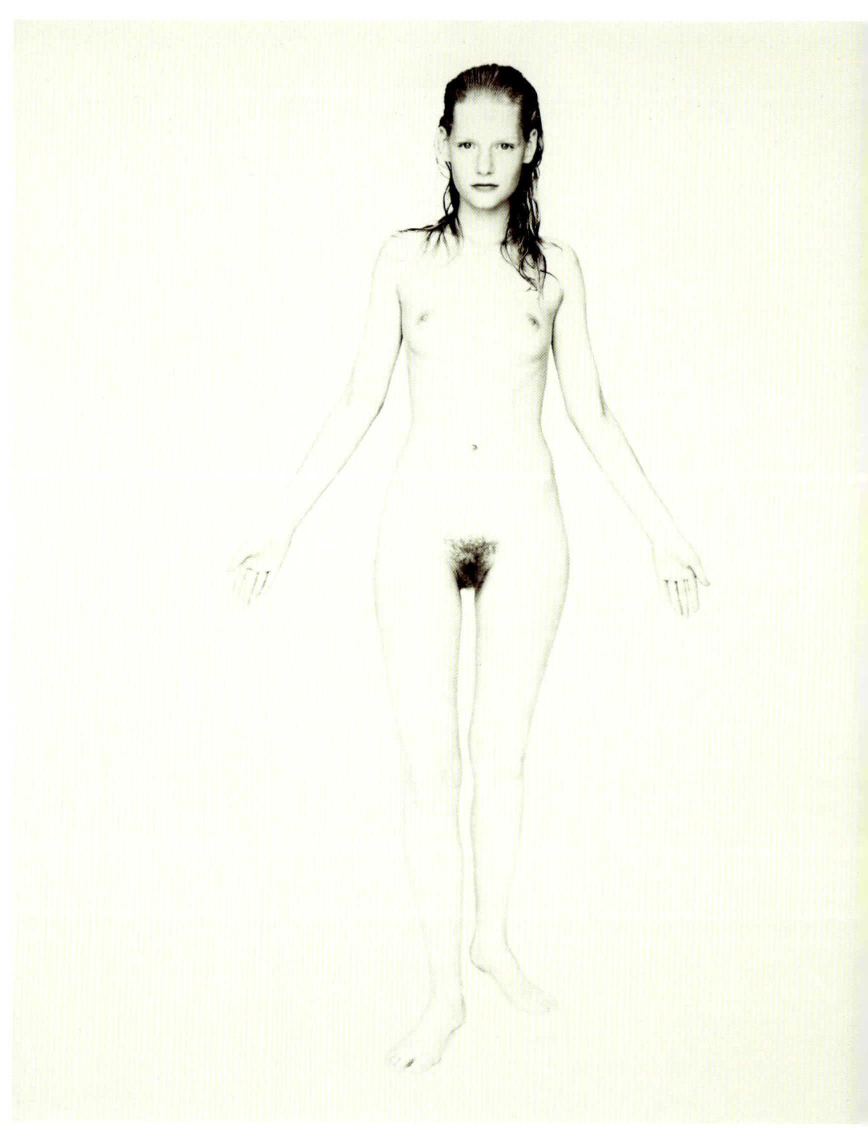

44. Kirsten, Paris, 1987.
45. Kate, Paris, 1992.

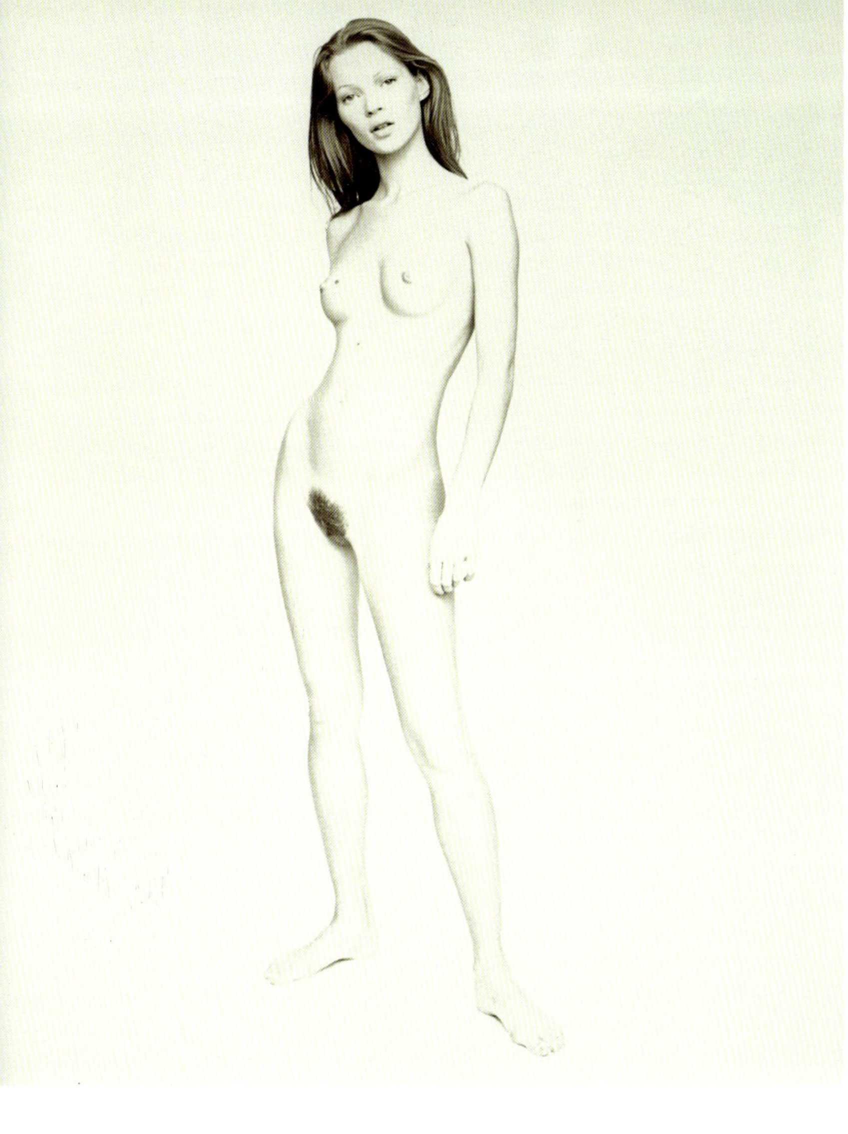

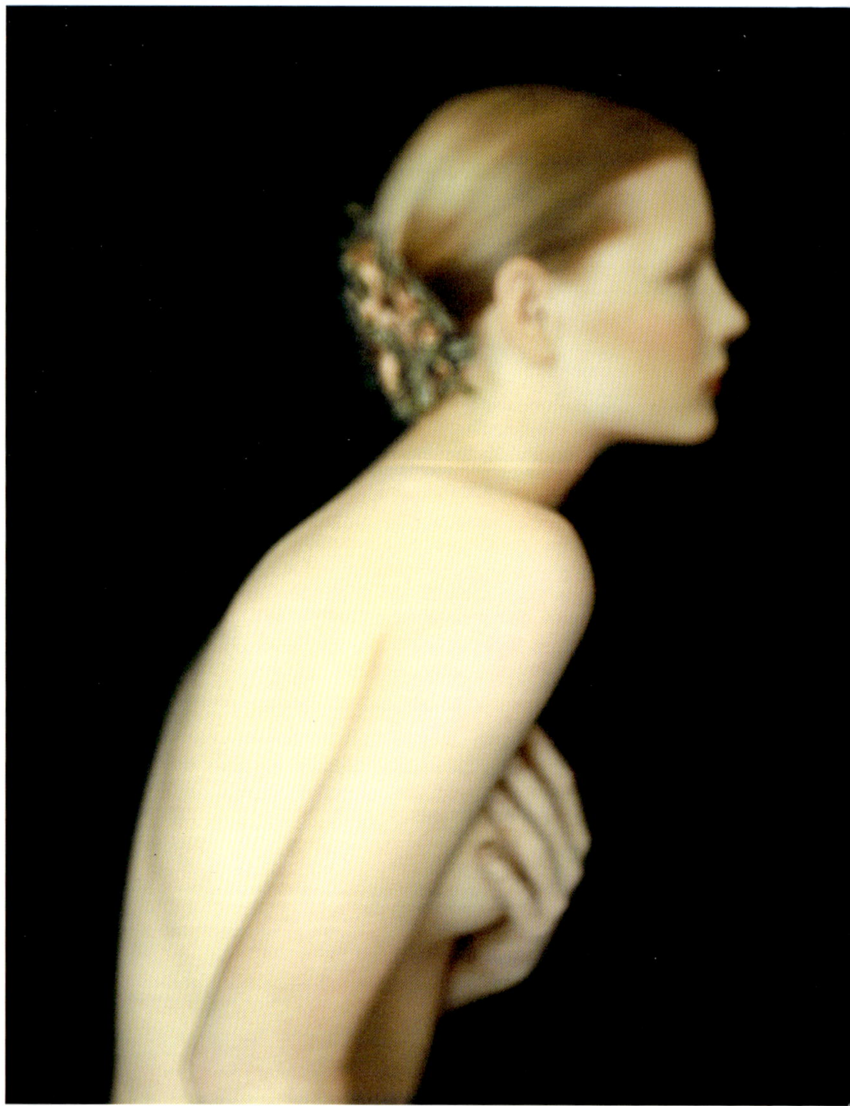

46 & 47. Kirsten, London, 1988.

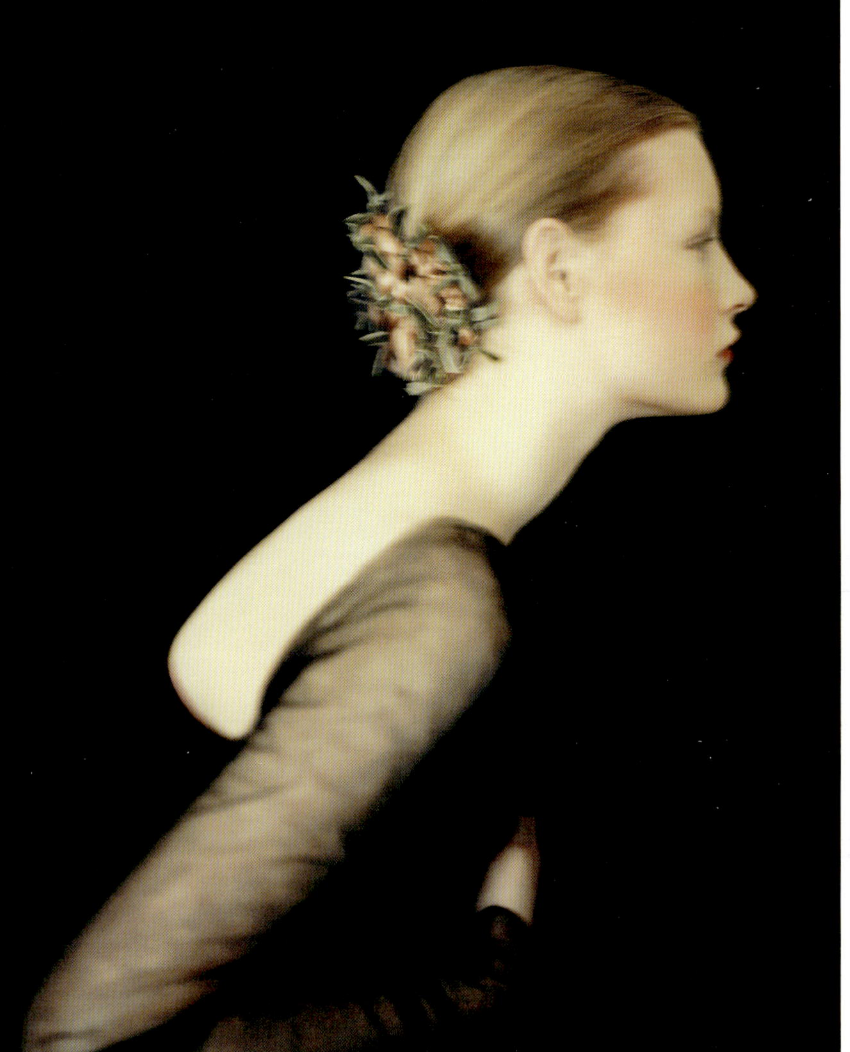

48. Anna, Tokyo, 2016.

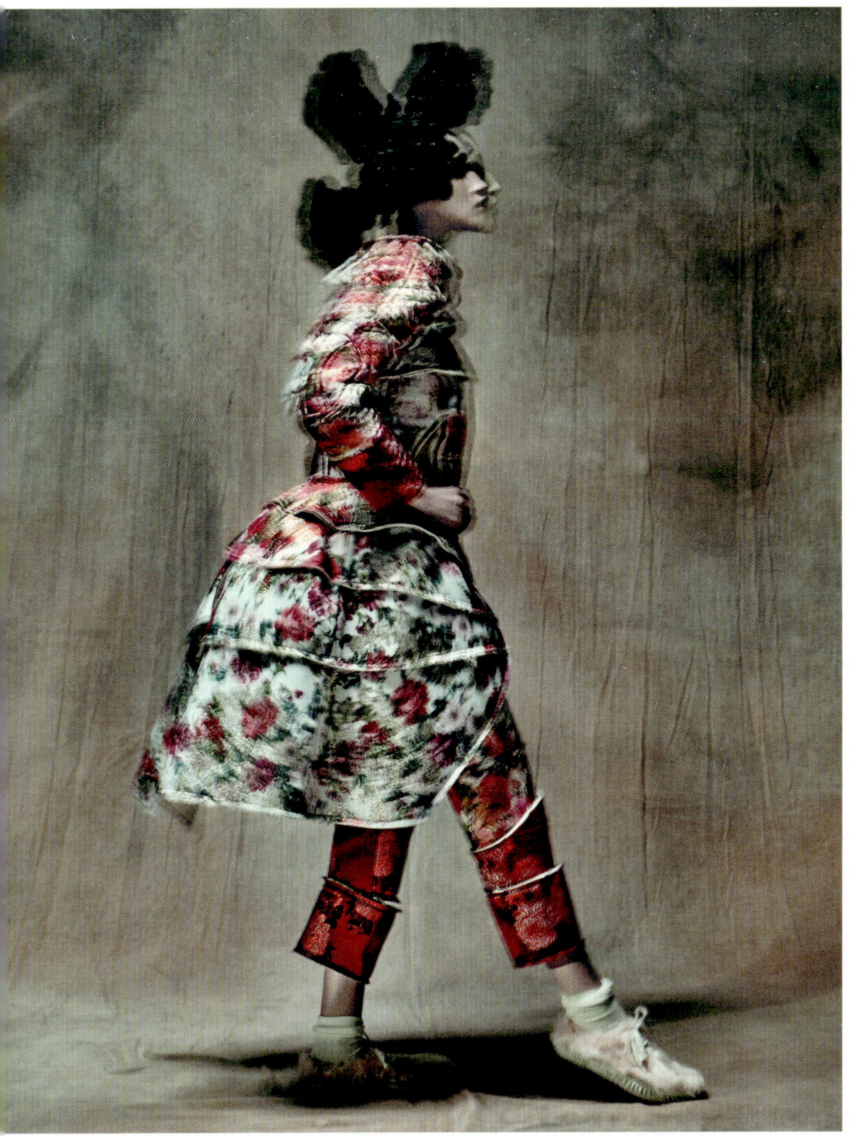

49. Gemma, New York, 2004.

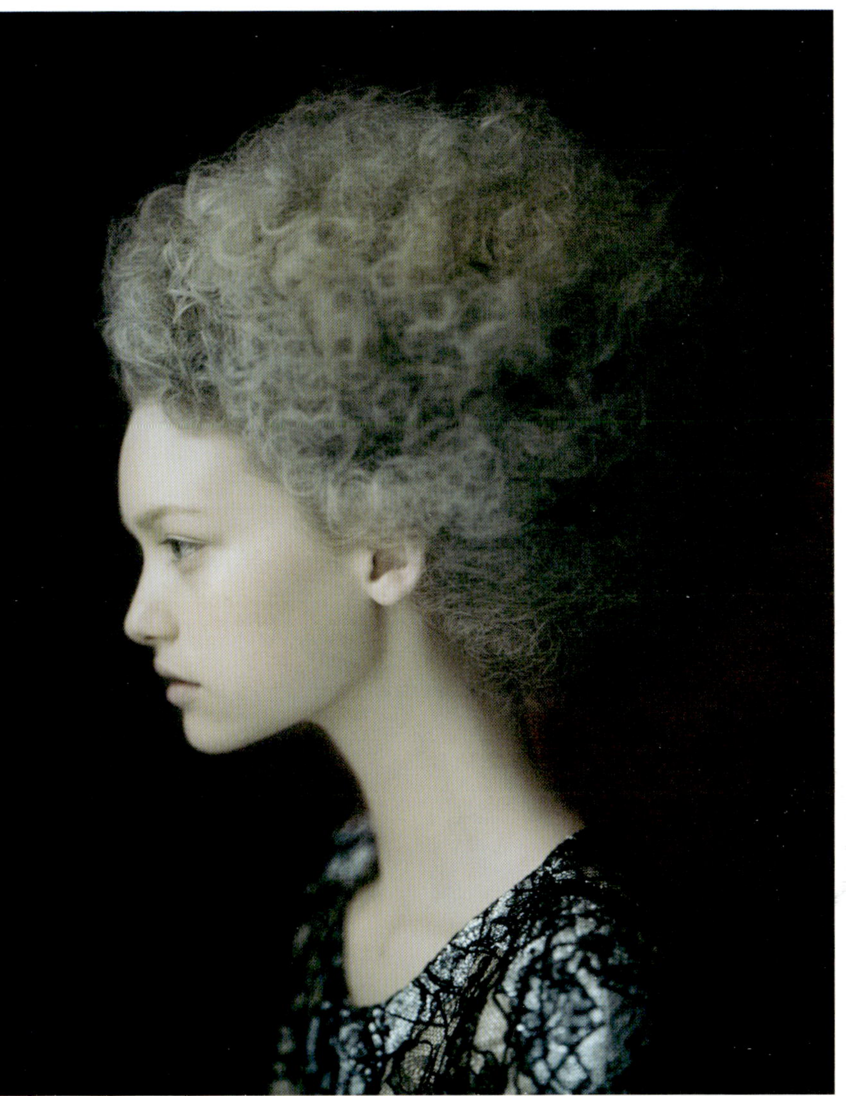

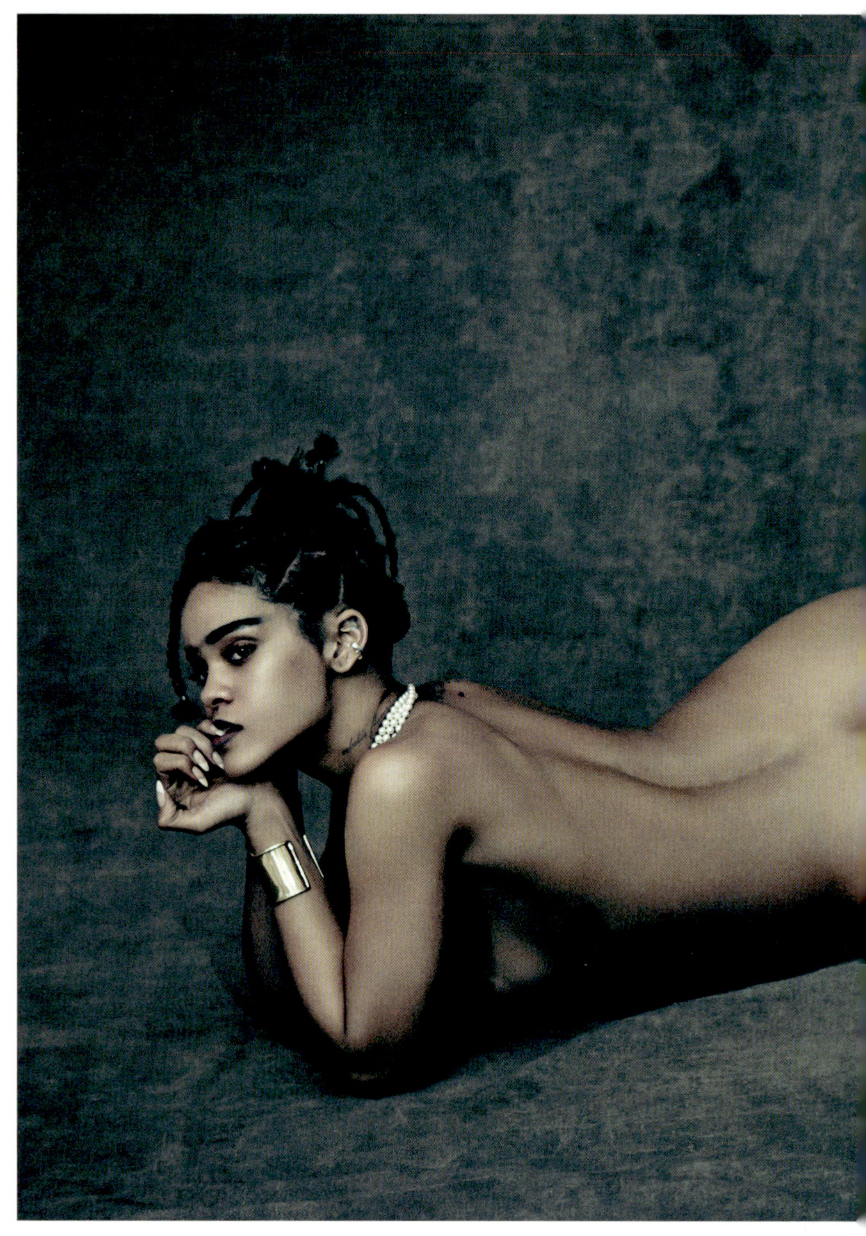

50. Rihanna, Paris, 2014.

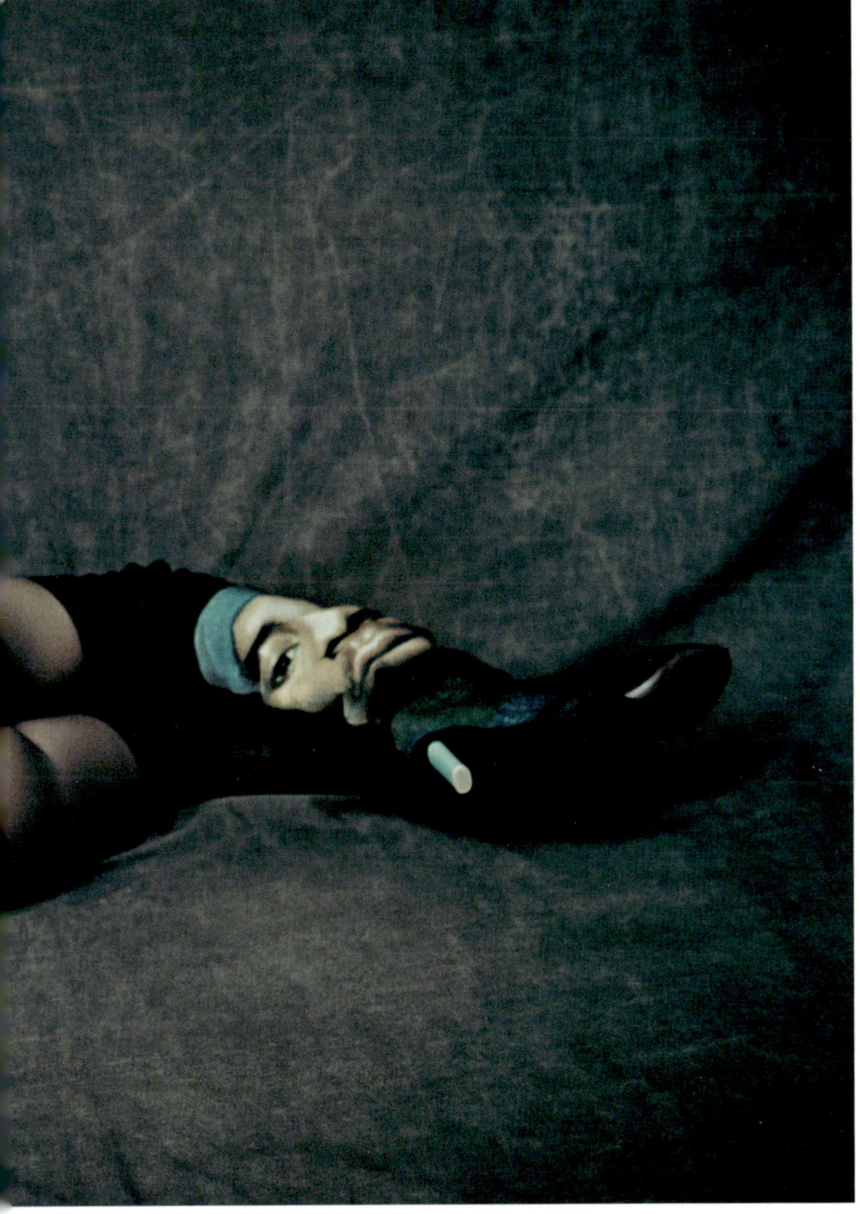

51. Kirsten, Paris, 1990.

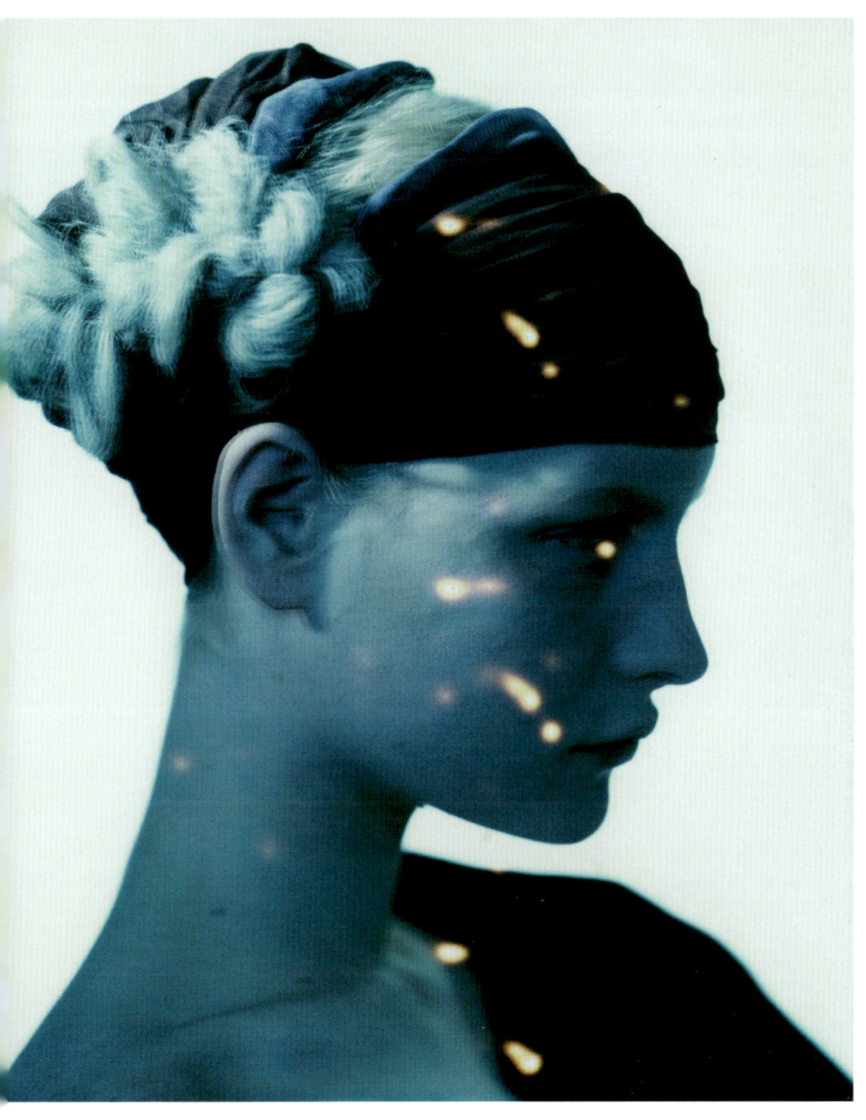

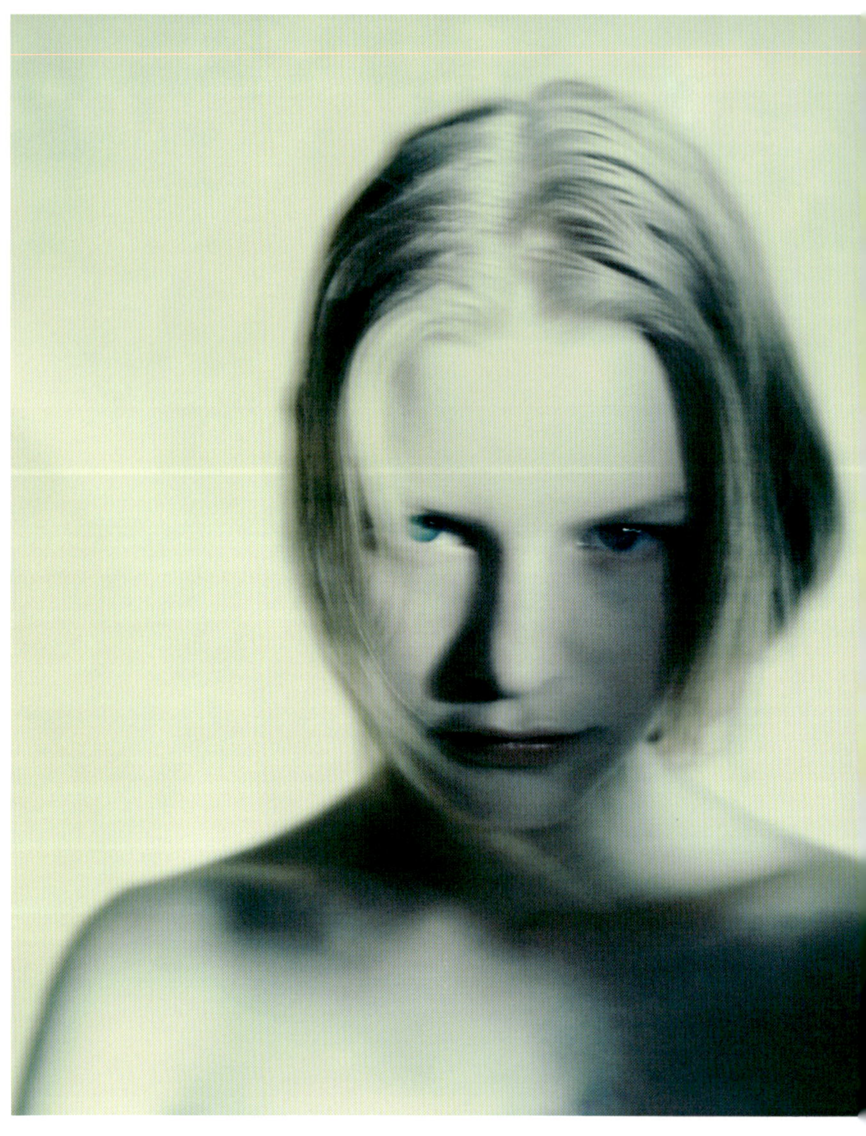

52 & 53. Kirsten, Paris, 1987.

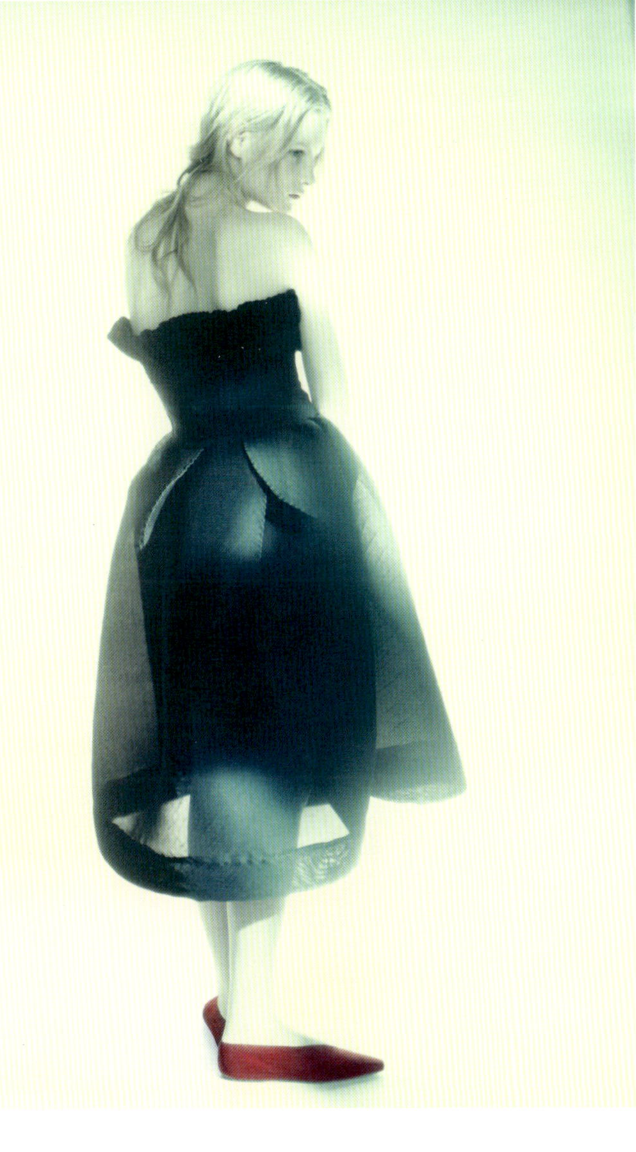

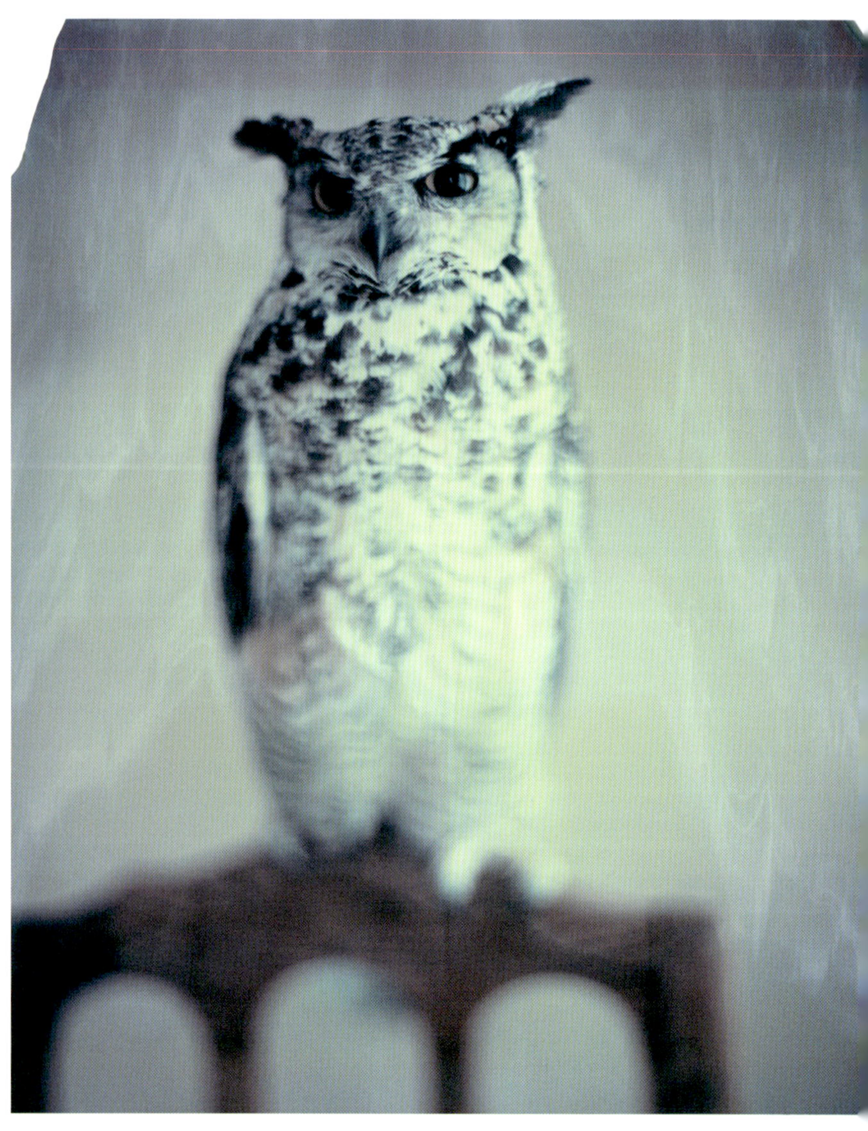

54. Owl, Paris, 2020.

55. Falcon, Paris, 2020.

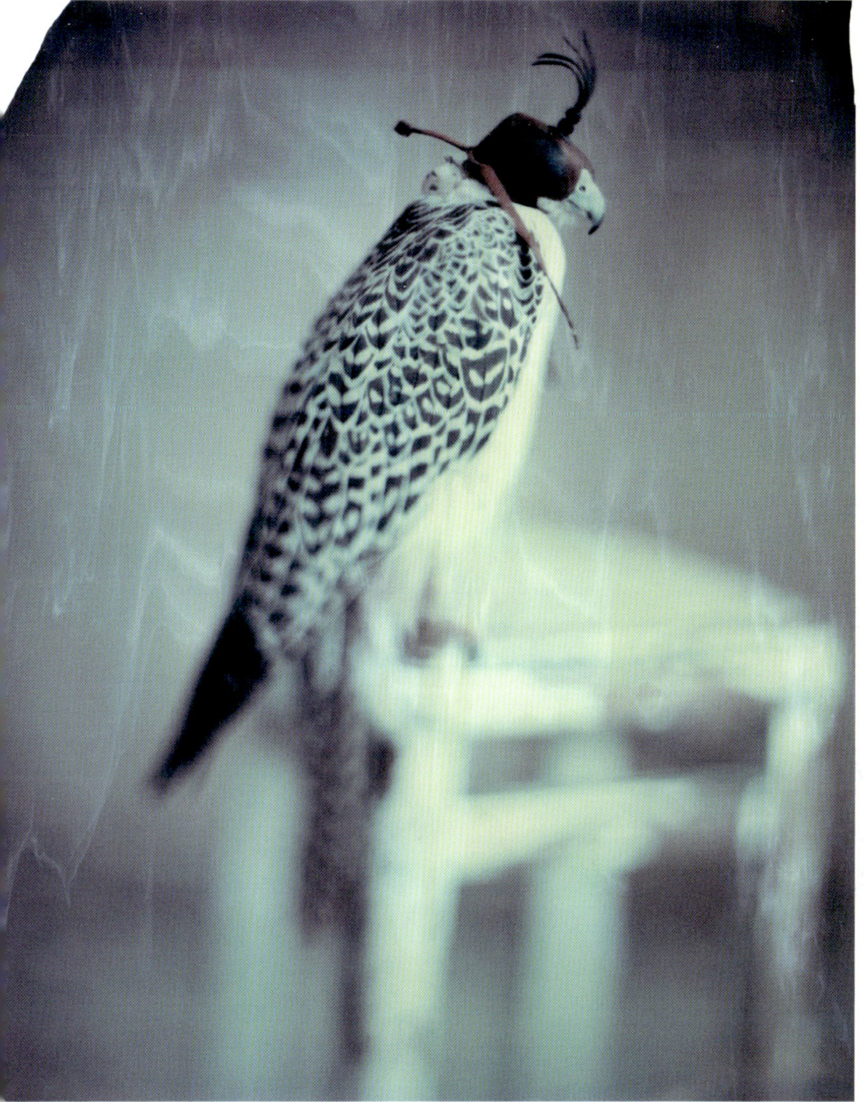

56. Anni, Paris, 2011.

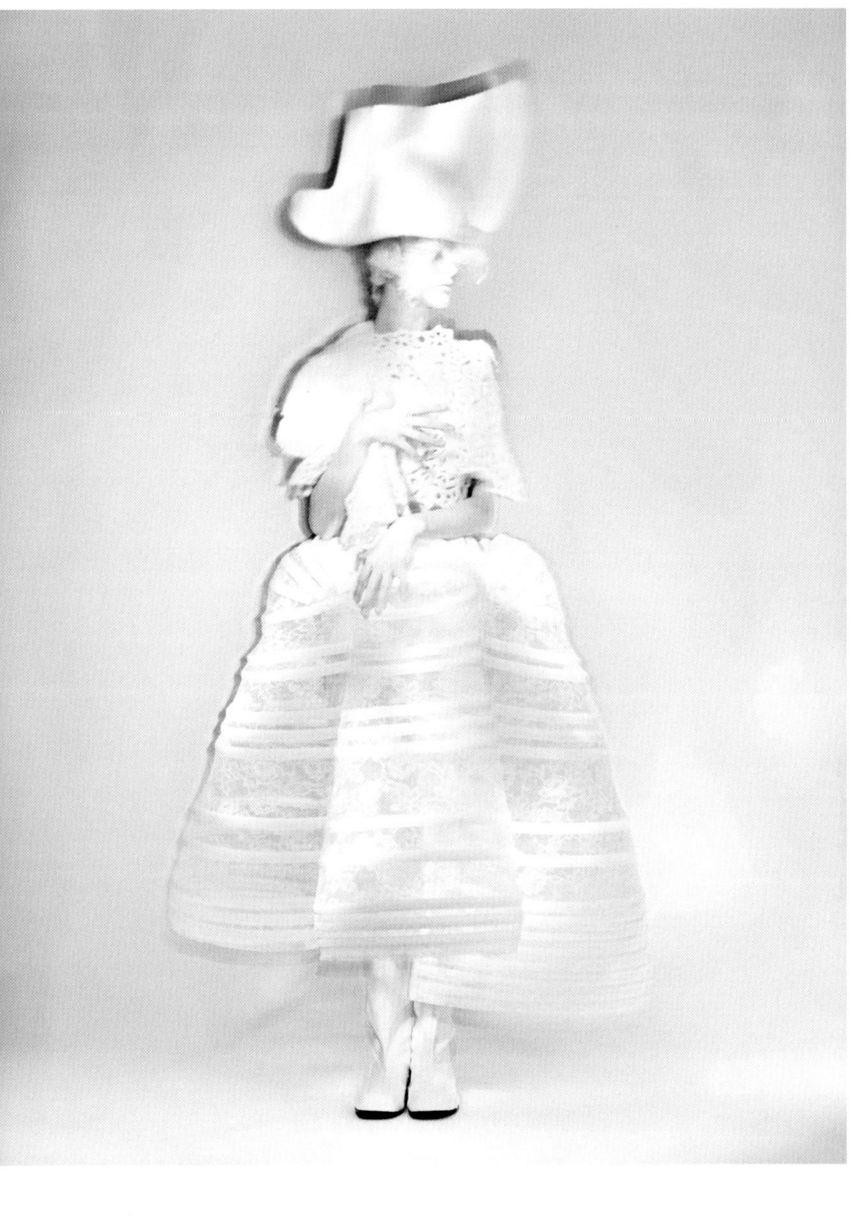

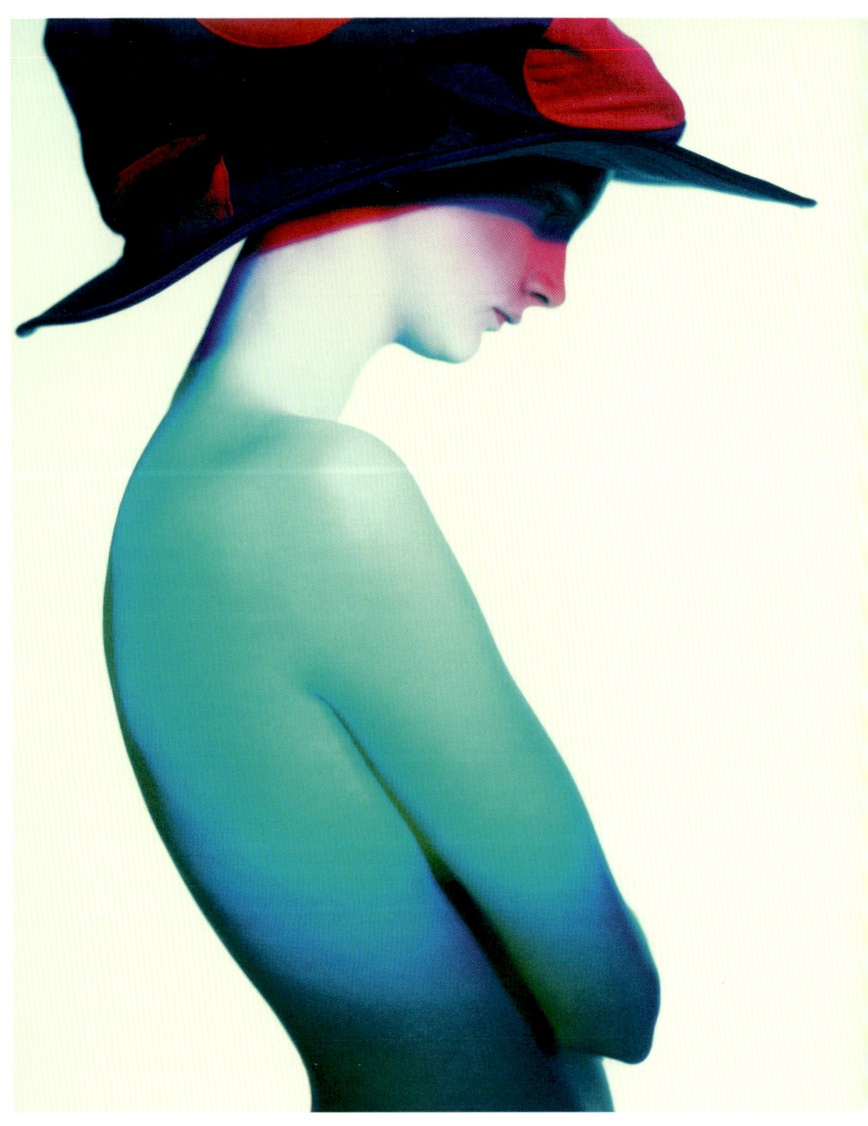

57 & 58. Sasha, Paris, 1985.

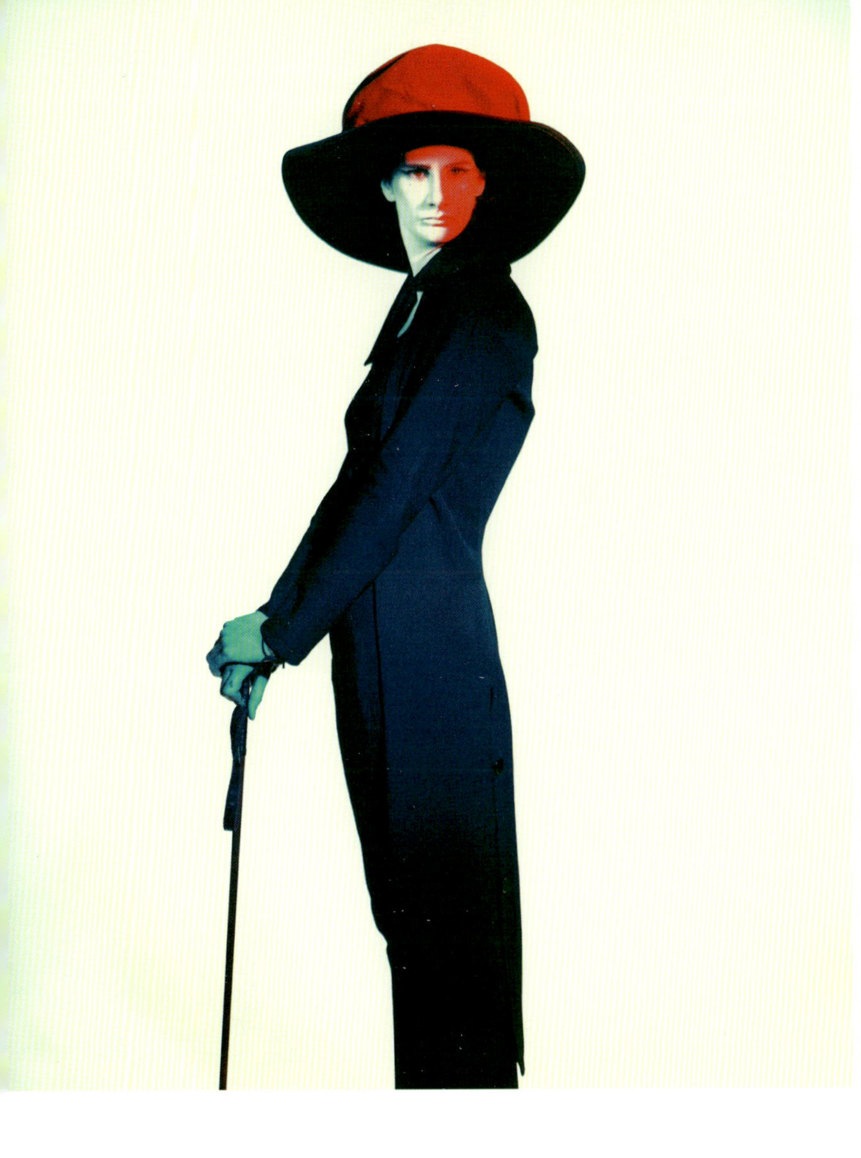

59. Audrey, Paris, 1996.

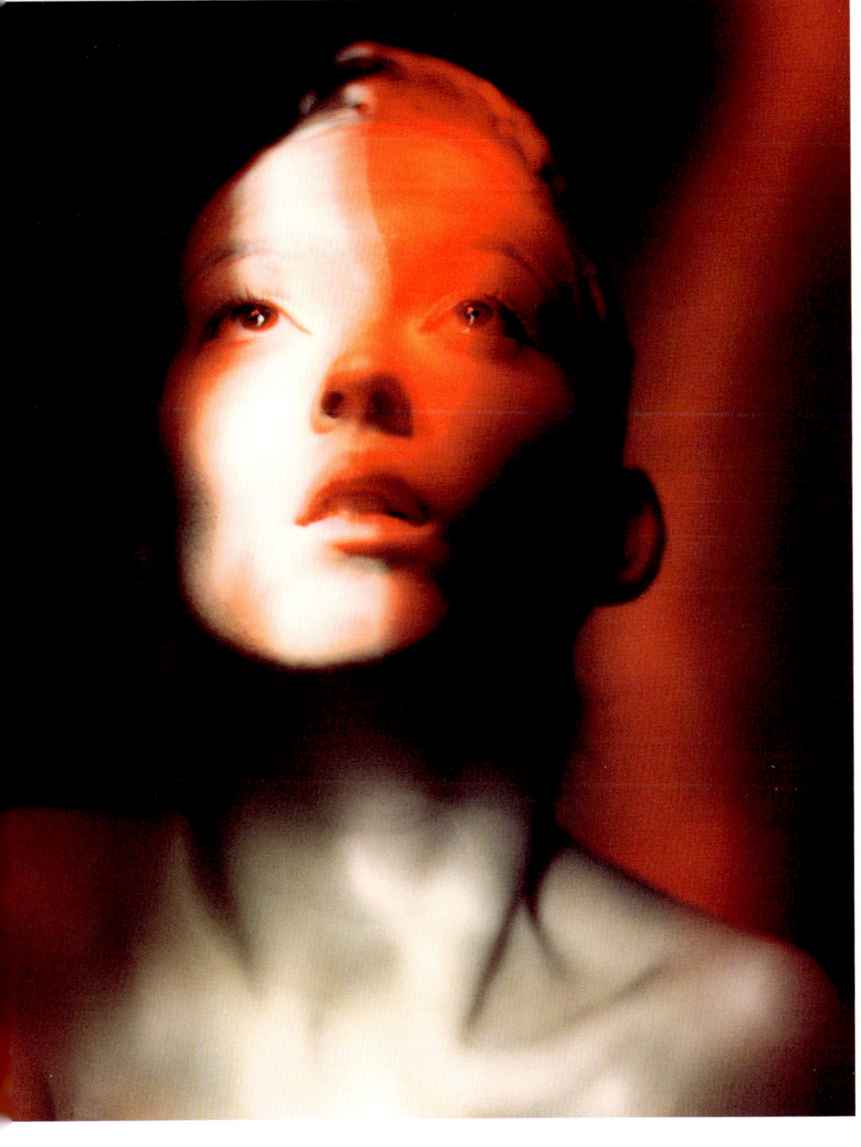

60. Molly, Paris, 2017.

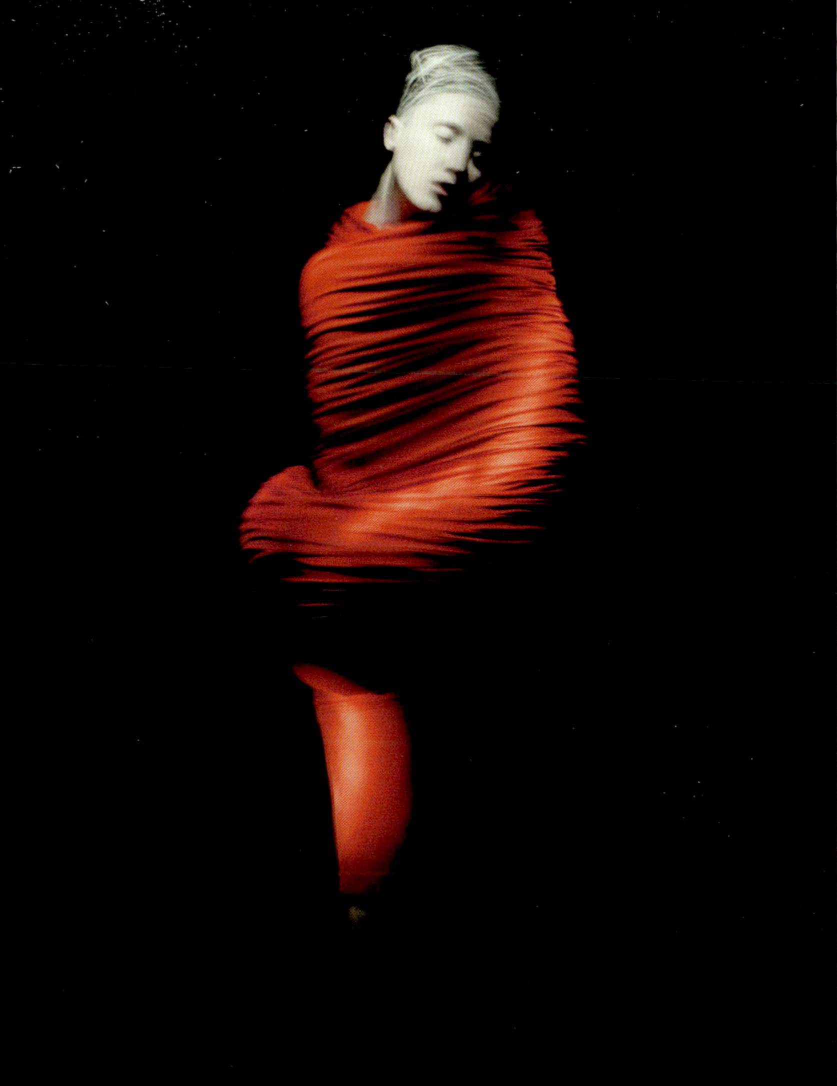

61. Guinevere, Paris, 2017.

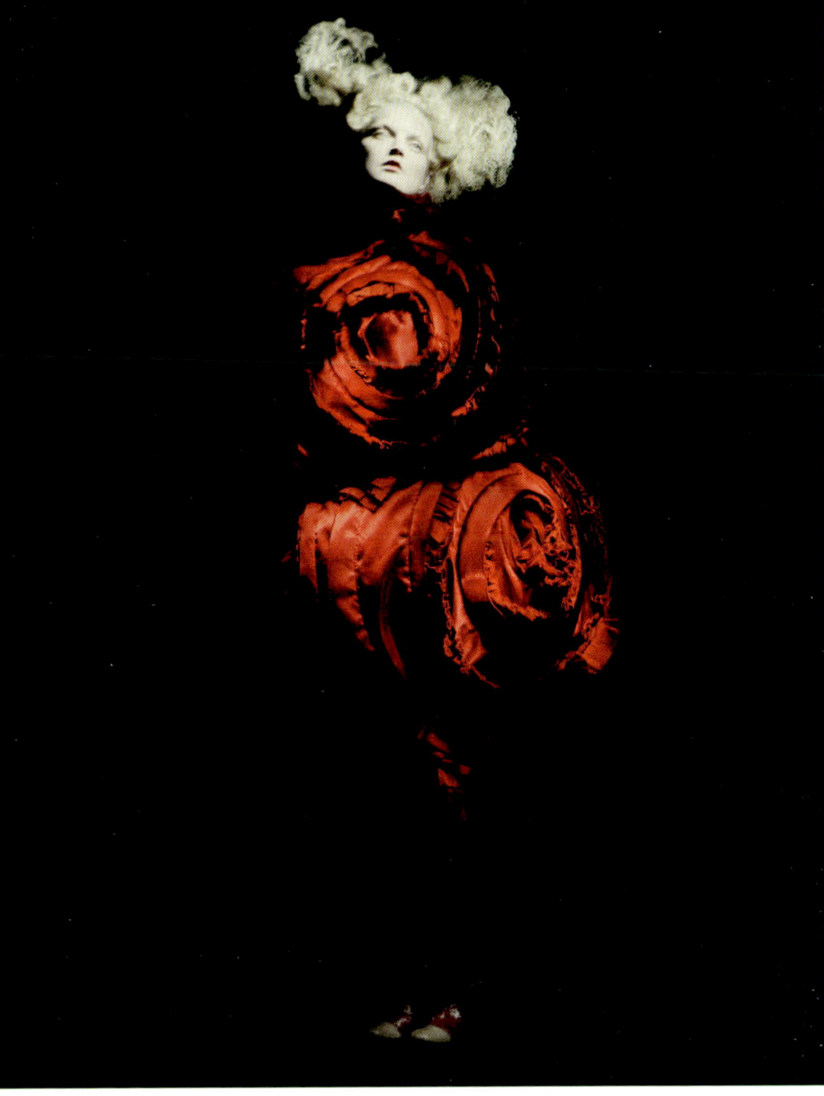

62. Audrey, Paris, 1996.

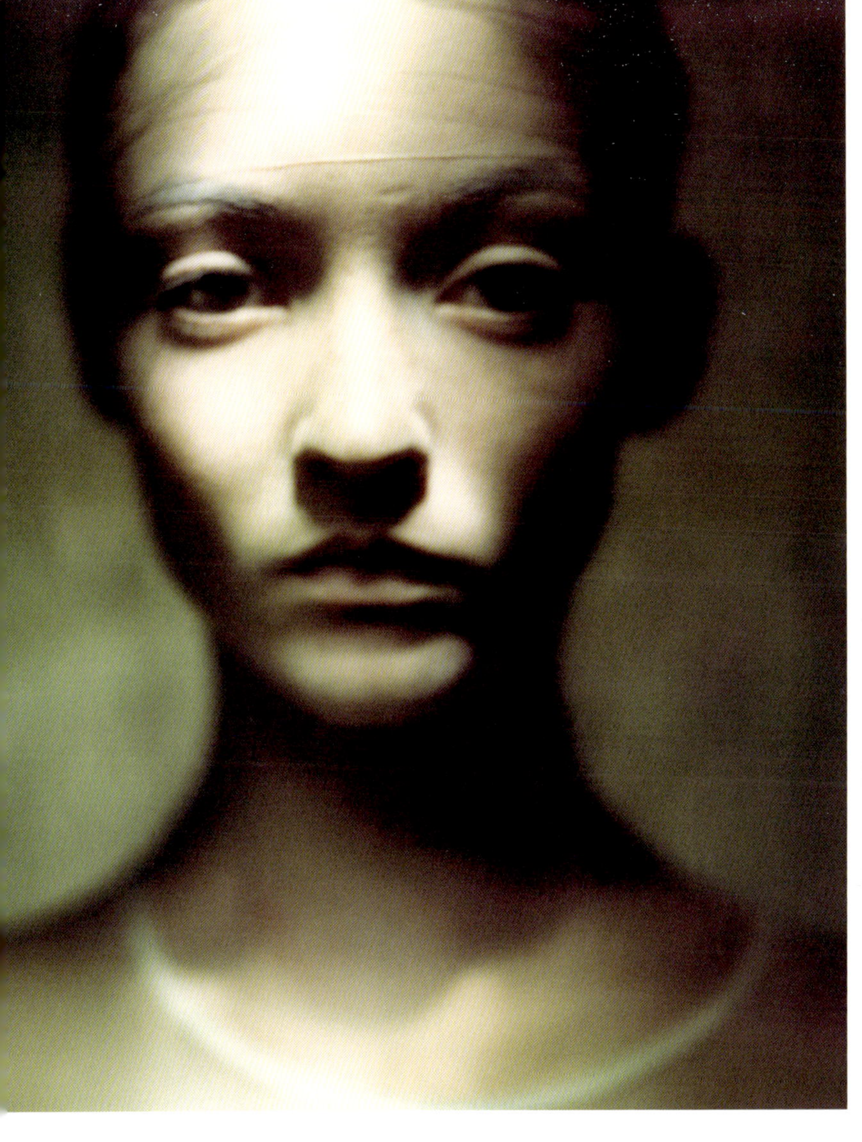

63. Sharon & Yelena, Paris, 1996.

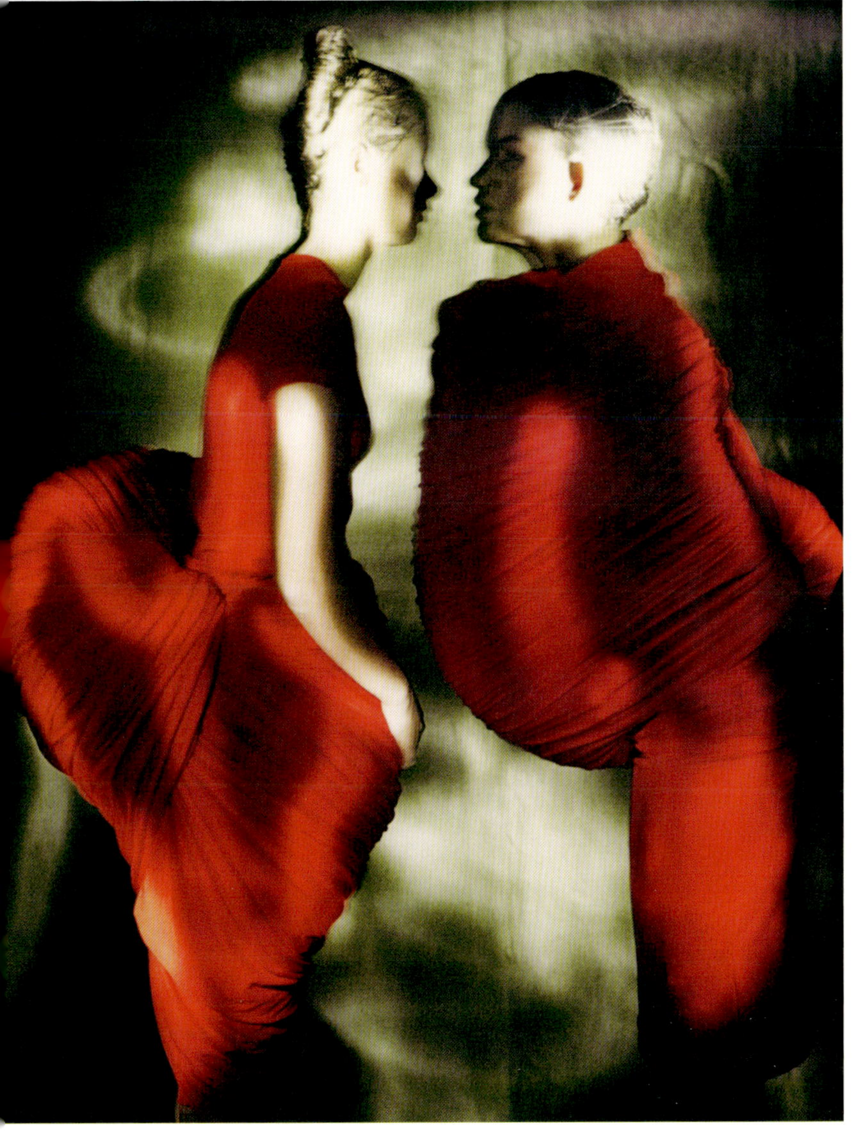

64. Audrey, Paris, 1996.

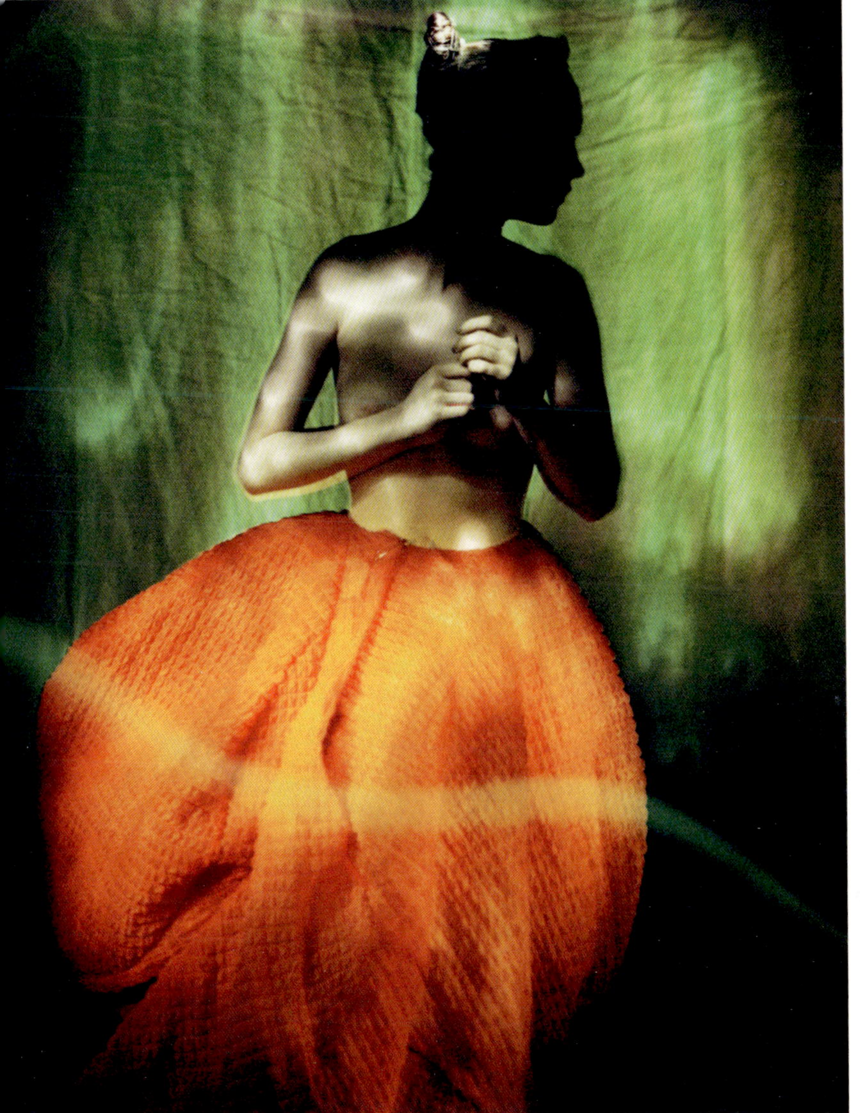

65. Audrey, Paris, 1996.

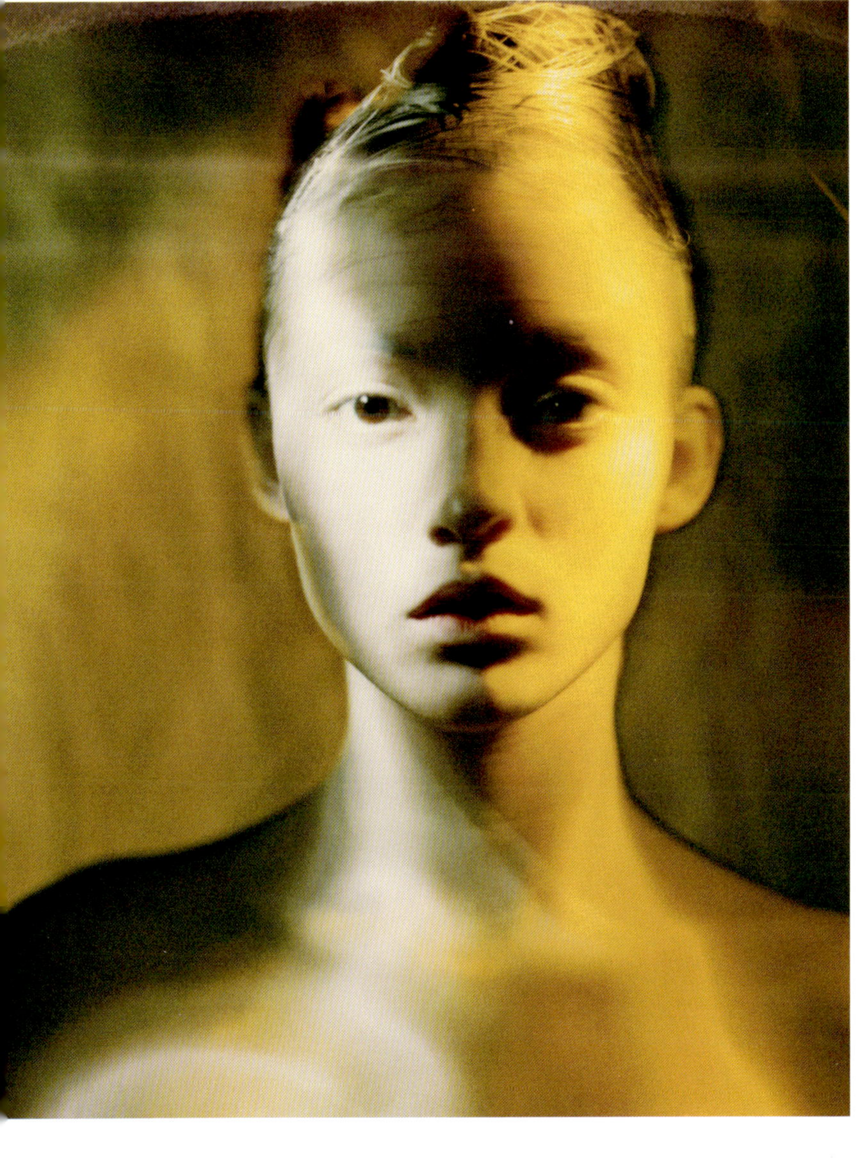

66. Guinevere, Paris, 1996.

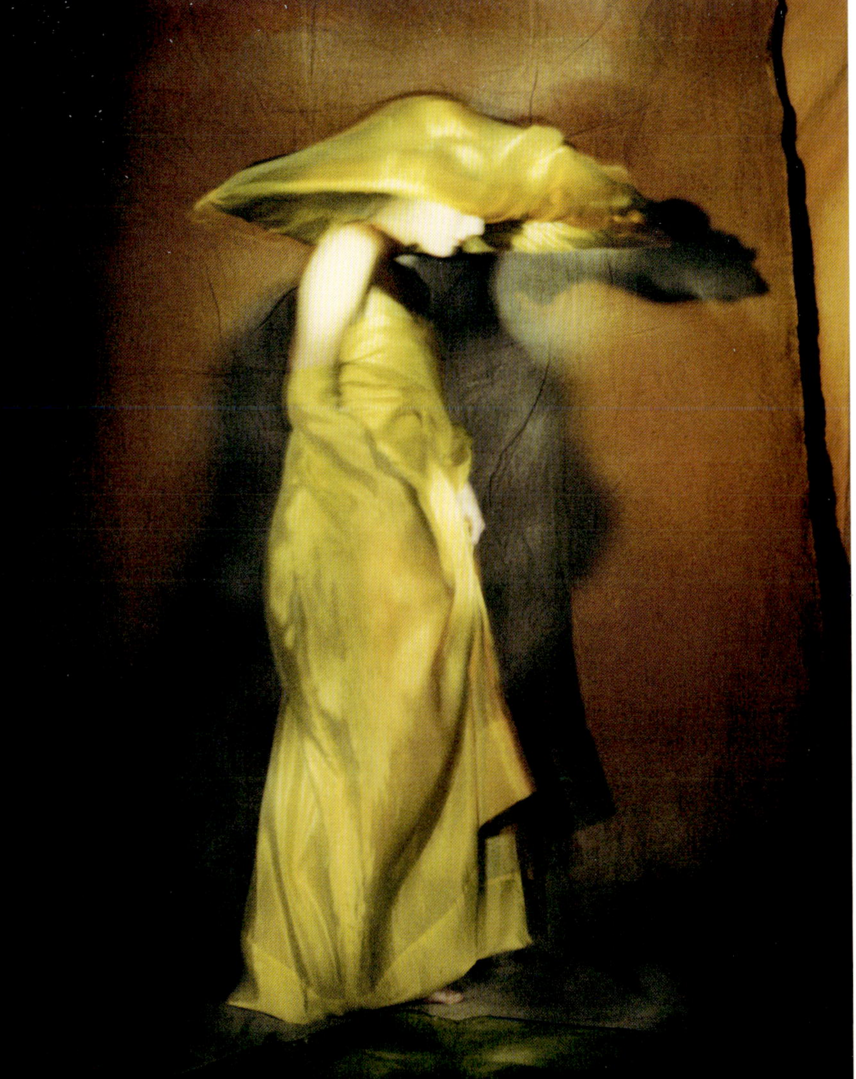

67. Molly, Paris, 2015.

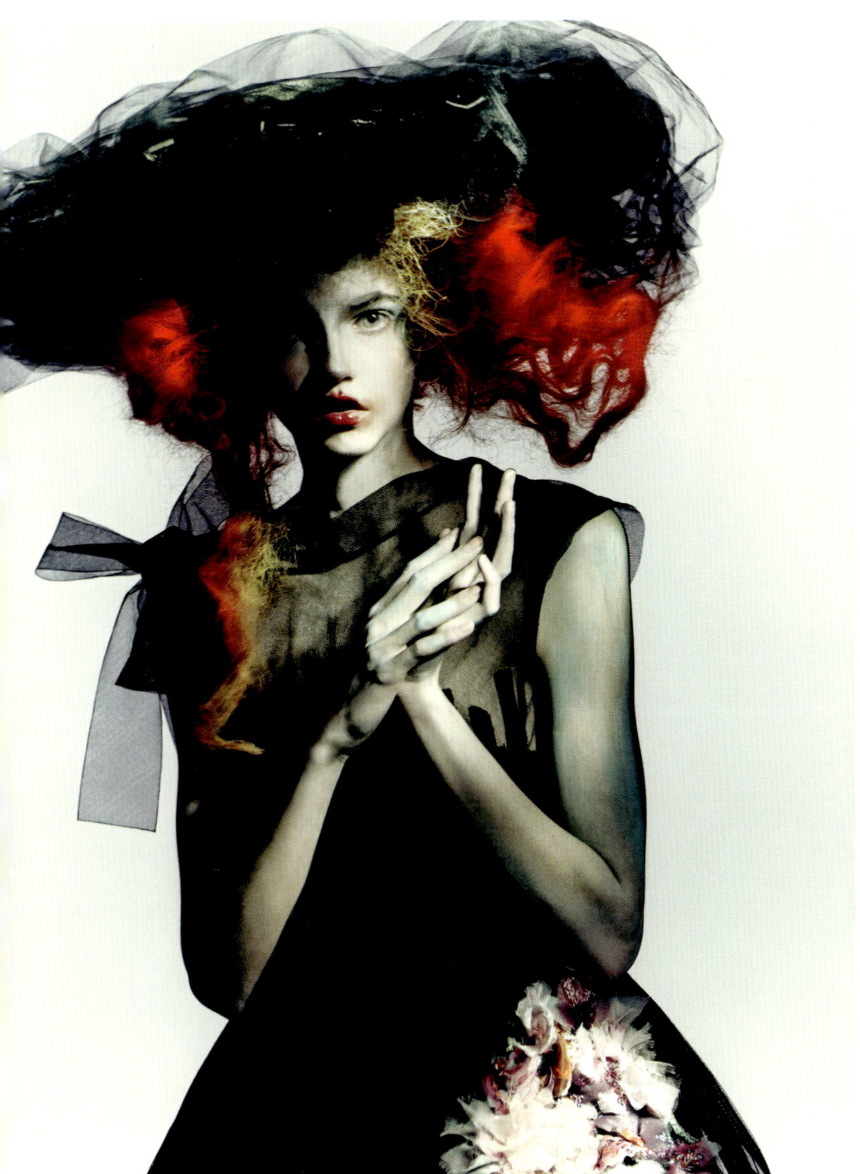

68. Sihana, Paris, 2023.

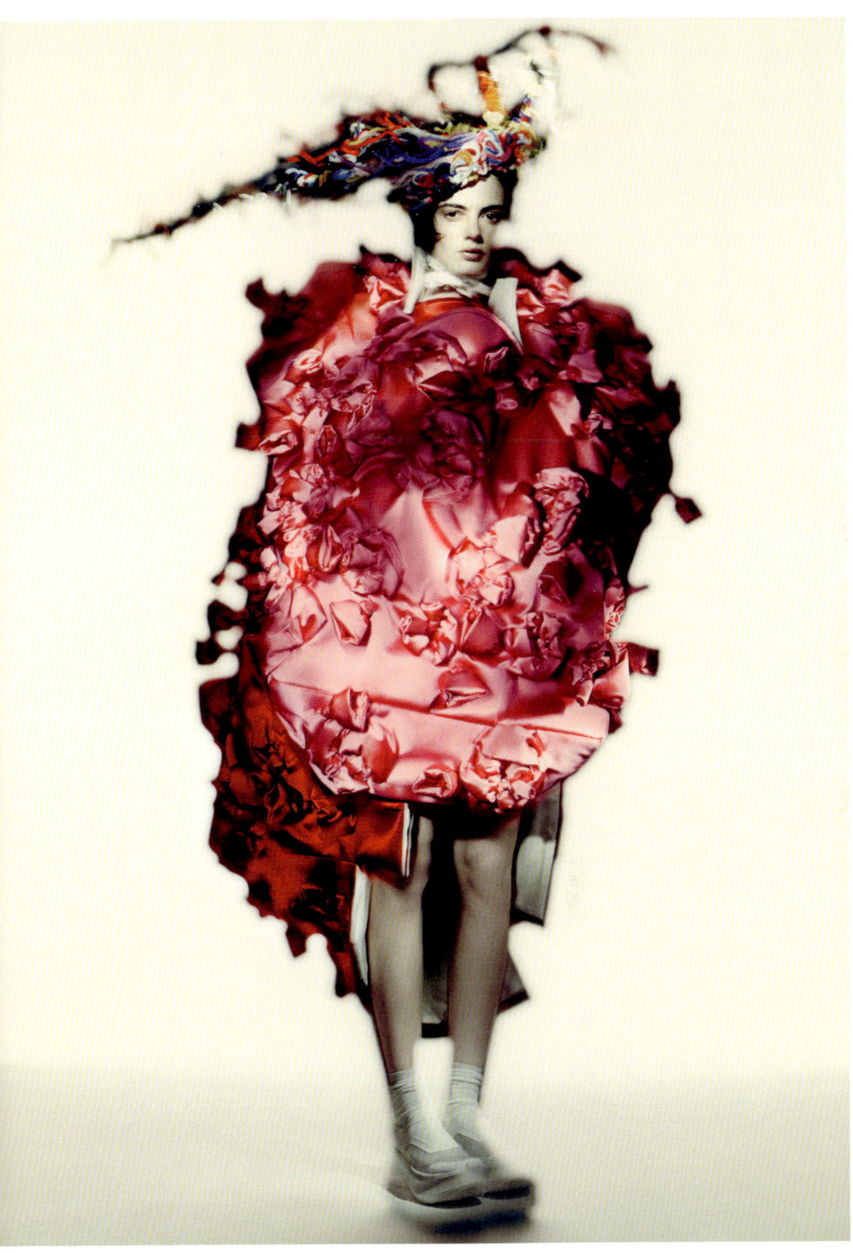

69. Roos, Paris, 2007.

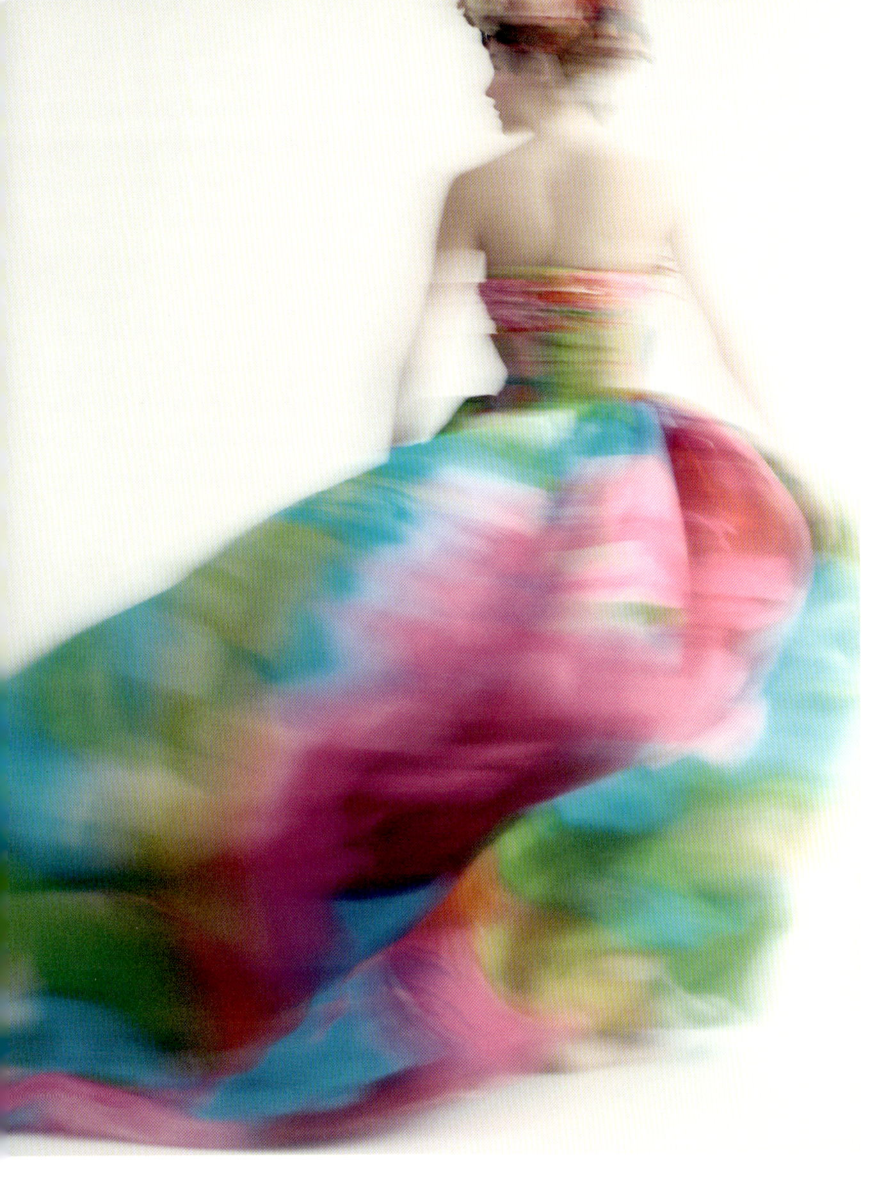

70. Roos, Paris, 2007.

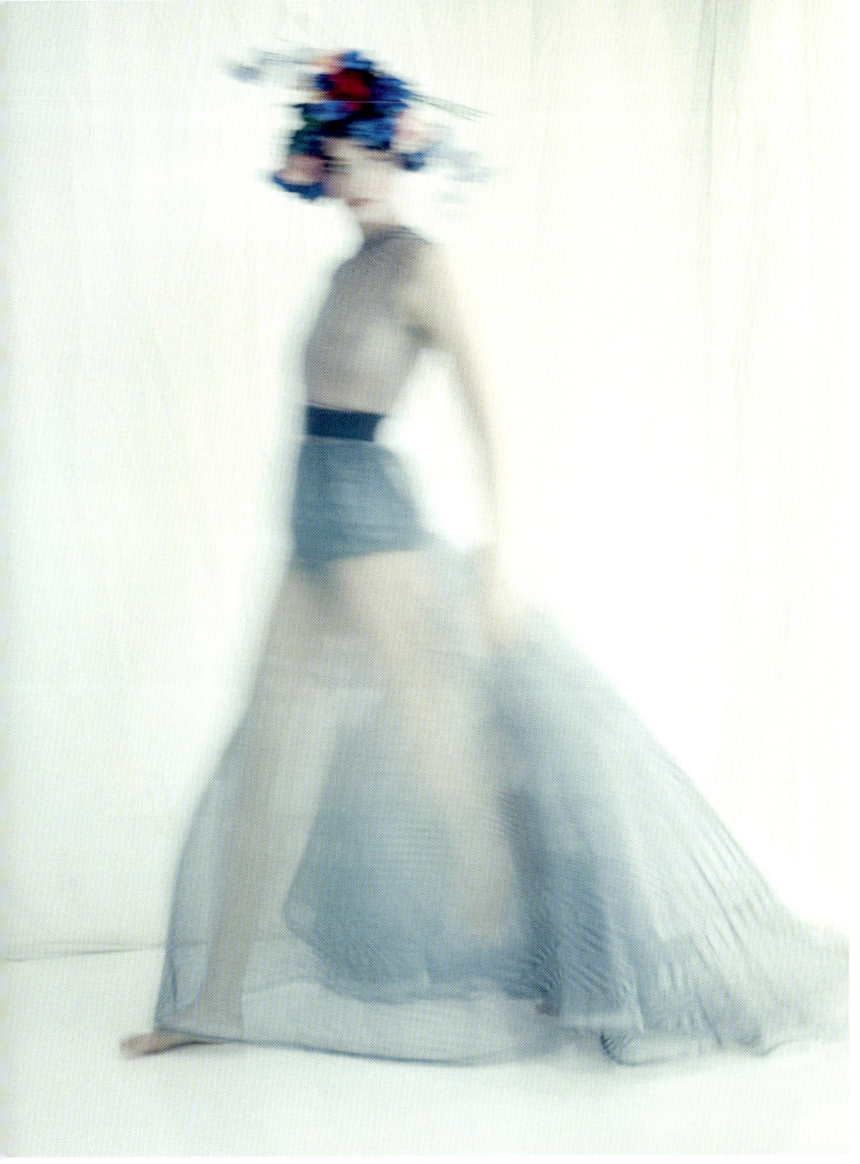

71. Sara Grace, Paris, 2018.

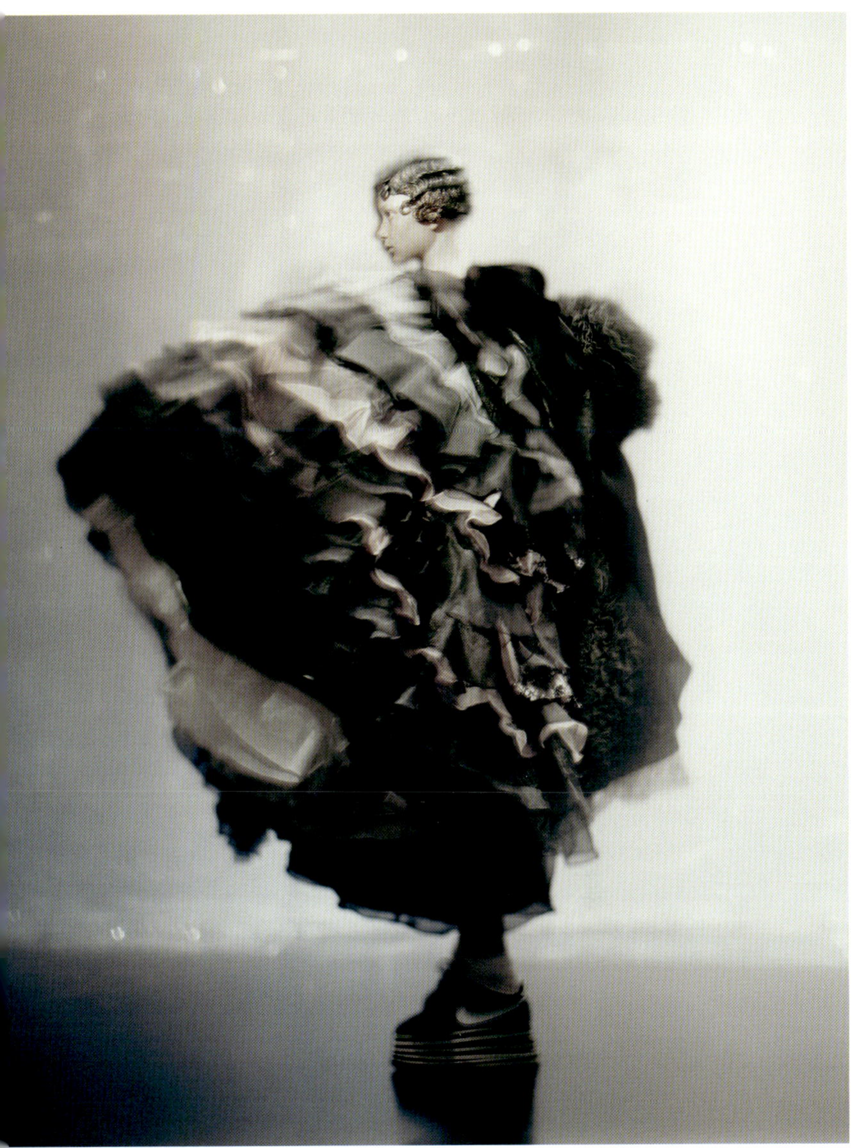

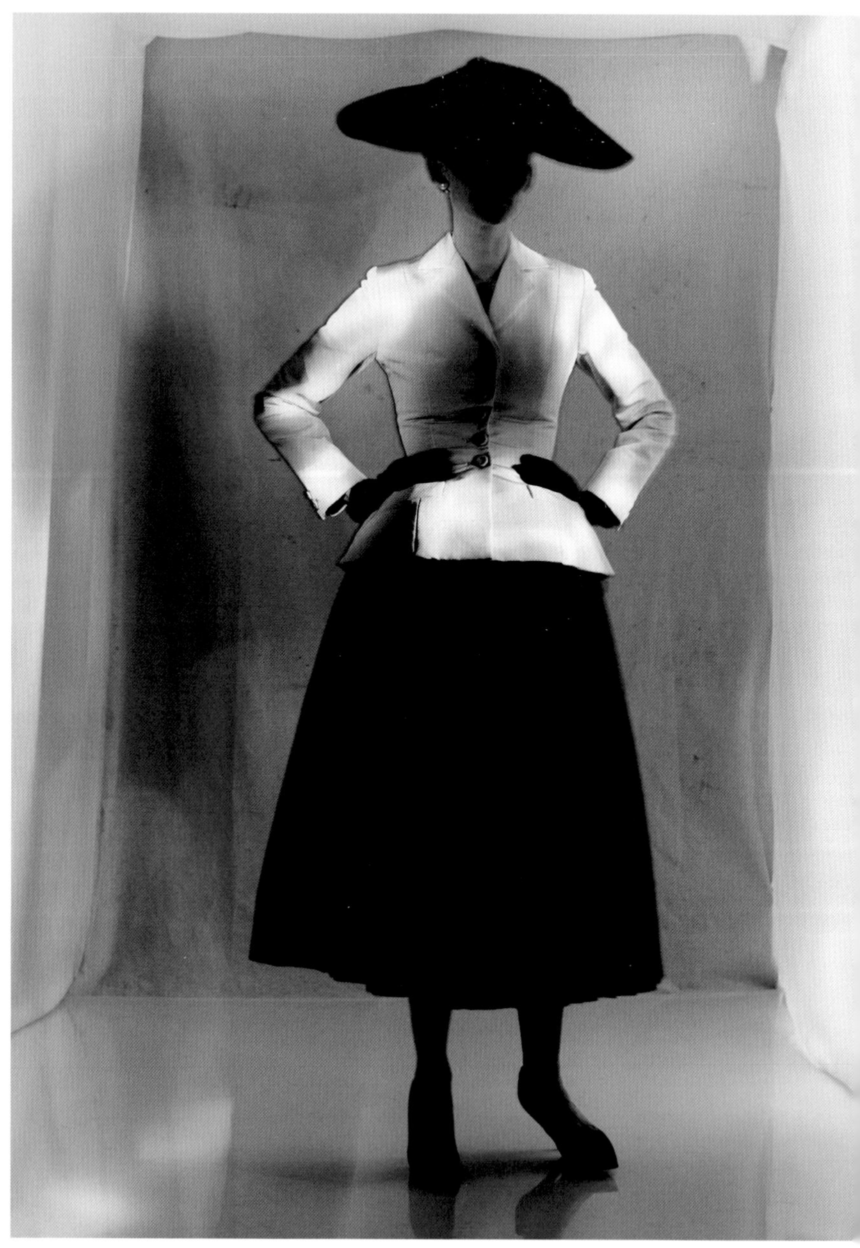

72. Audrey, Paris, 2016.

Biography

I arrived in Paris one November evening in 1973. In the driving rain, I looked for a hotel: Hôtel Namur, rue Delambre, 19 francs a night. One afternoon, I invited a pretty girl over; I moved the bed and my first Paris studio was born.

Rue Delambre meant the Pictorial Service labs, and Jean-Paul Sartre and Simone de Beauvoir on the terrace of La Coupole. My friend Popy Moreni introduced me to the world of fashion, and I looked for a position as an assistant. I went to see Helmut Newton, then Guy Bourdin at his studio on the rue des Ecouffes, who told me: 'Don't go to New York, it's a photographers' graveyard.' Then Laurence Sackman hired me as an assistant and taught me everything.

As the days went by, I slowly became a photographer. In my kitchen at night, I took still lifes and built up a portfolio. My first shots were published by *Depeche Mode*, *Elle* and *Marie Claire*. One night in 1980 at the Pin-Up Studio, I discovered 8 × 10 Polaroids, and it was love at first sight. I bought my first Deardorff camera in New York and my life in large format began...

I've been lucky enough to meet some amazing people and to collaborate with some of them; many muses have inspired my work, each one with her own personality and unique beauty. When I look back, all I see is an intimate diary, written day after day, with a great deal of love and passion.

Since the rue Delambre, I've always lived on the Left Bank and have moved house several times, each home also serving as my studio, until I found the place on the rue Paul Fort which has now been my studio for years. I love Paris; the city has given me everything and taught me everything, but sometimes I miss the mists of Ravenna, even more so than the sunshine of the Adriatic. I was born there in 1947 and grew up with the Byzantine mosaics and the wonderful cookies from the Mariuccia bakery. I don't know why I became such a nostalgic romantic; perhaps it was those biscuits, or simply the marvellous childhood I spent there.

As a teenager, I loved poetry, I read a lot of it and also tried to write it, then I grew to love theatre, then film, and later, during a trip to Spain in 1966, photography. Back in Ravenna, I turned the cellar into a darkroom and spent my first nights with my hands in the developer, the stop bath, the fixer, those names with their symbolic alchemy. I saw the image slowly form on the light-sensitive paper and I was captivated for ever and ever.

P.S. 1947 was also the year that Polaroids were born. Dr Edwin Land's wonderful invention allowed me to feed and enrich my palette and my imagination, as it did for hundreds of other photographers and millions of people all over the world. I consider it an enormous cultural and artistic loss that this magical and unique film has been taken out of production.

Paolo Roversi

Selected bibliography

Una donna, Milan: Carla Sozzani, 1989

Donne Nude, portfolio, Tokyo, 1990

Angeli, exh. cat., Paris: Galerie Camera Obscura, 1993

Paolo Roversi, exh. cat., Toulouse: Galerie Municipale du Château d'Eau, 1994

Al-Mukalla, Paris: Galerie Camera Obscura, 1995

Nudi, Paris: Éditions Stromboli, 1999

Images Cerruti, Göttingen: Steidl, 1999

Libretto, Paris: Éditions Stromboli, 2000

Studio, Göttingen: Steidl/Dangin, 2009

Paolo Roversi: Photofile, London: Thames & Hudson, 2011

Secrets, Paris: Éditions Stromboli, 2013

Natalia, Paris: Éditions Stromboli, 2017

Storie, exh. cat., Milan: Palazzo Reale/Skira, 2017

Dior Images – Paolo Roversi, text by Emanuele Coccia, New York: Rizzoli, 2018

Looking for Juliet: The 2020 Pirelli Calendar photographed by Paolo Roversi, Milan: Pirelli, 2019

Studio Luce, Paris: Éditions Stromboli, 2020

Tris, Paris: Éditions Stromboli, 2020

Birds, Paris: Éditions Stromboli, 2020

Paolo Roversi, Rome: Contrasto, 2021

Paolo Roversi par Christian Caujolle, Marseille: André Frères Éditions, 2022

Des oiseaux, Paris: Atelier EXB/Éditions Xavier Barral, 2023

Lettres sur la lumière, with Emanuele Coccia, text by Chiara Bardelli-Nonino and Erri De Luca, Paris: Gallimard, 2024

Paolo Roversi, Paris: Paris Musées, 2024; English ed. London: Thames & Hudson, 2025

Selected exhibitions

1989 'Una donna', Solomon Gallery, New York;
Spazio Romeo Gigli, Milan.

1990 'Donne Nude', Tokyo.

1992 International Festival of Fashion
Photography, Monaco.

1993–94 'Angeli', Photo Gallery International,
Tokyo; Galerie Camera Obscura, Paris.

1995 'Paris défile', Galerie Brownstone, Paris.
'Polaroids', Hamiltons Gallery, London.

1997 Comme des Garçons, Tokyo.
'Fashion', Scalo Bookshop, Zurich
(with Robert Frank).

1998 'Portraits', Galerie 213, Paris.

2000 'Photographs', Galleria Carla Sozzani,
Milan.

2001 'Images. Cerruti', James Gallery, Moscow.

2002 'Studio', Pace/MacGill Gallery, New York;
Galerie Camera Obscura, Paris.

2005 'Studio', Transphotographiques, Lille.

2006 'Studio', Yokohama Red Brick Warehouse
No. 1, Yokohama.

2007 National Art Museum of China, Beijing;
Shanghai Art Museum; Guangdong Museum
of Art, Guangzhou.

2008 'Guinevere', Pace/MacGill Gallery,
New York.
'Studio', Les Rencontres d'Arles.

2009 Camera Work, Berlin; Atelier Jungwirth,
Graz.

2010 'Studio', Biennale 'Vive la France',
Moscow House of Photography, Moscow;
Kunsthalle, Rostock.

2012 'Baci', Silencio, Paris.
Tashkent House of Photography.
The Wapping Project Bankside, London.
'Photographs', Galleria Carla Sozzani, Milan.
'Studio', Cloister of San Pietro, Reggio Emilia.

2013–14 'Secrets', Galerie Camera Obscura,
Paris; Fotografiska, Stockholm.

2015 'Polaroids', Hamiltons Gallery, London.

2017 'Storie', Photo Vogue Festival, Palazzo
Reale, Milan.
'Incontri', Fondazione Sozzani, Milan.

2018 'Photographs', Shoot Gallery, Oslo.

2019 'Intangible Presence', Fahey/Klein
Gallery, Los Angeles.
'Doubts', Pace/MacGill Gallery, New York.

2020 'Looking for Juliet', Multimedia Art
Museum, Moscow.
'Studio Luce', Museo d'Arte della Città di
Ravenna, Ravenna.
'Birds', Dallas Contemporary.

2022 'Portraits', Galerie Camera Obscura,
Paris.
'Nudi', Palazzo Baronio, Ravenna.

2023 'India', Galerie Leica, Paris.

2024 'Paolo Roversi', Palais Galliera, Paris.

The Photofile series is the original English-language edition of the Photo Poche collection. It was first published between 1986 and 1992 by the Centre National de la Photographie, Paris, with the support of the French Ministry of Culture. Robert Delpire (1926–2017) was the creator of the series and its managing editor until 2017.

General editor: Géraldine Lay
Series design by Matthew Young
Translated from the Italian and French

First published in the United Kingdom in 2011 by
Thames & Hudson Ltd, 181A High Holborn, London WC1V 7QX

First published in the United States of America in 2011 by
Thames & Hudson Inc., 500 Fifth Avenue, New York, New York 10110

British Library Cataloguing-in-Publication Data
A catalogue record for this book is available from the British Library

Library of Congress Catalog Card Number 2024946255

ISBN: 978-0-500-41130-8

Impression 01

Printed and bound in Italy

Be the first to know about our new releases, exclusive content and author events by visiting
thamesandhudson.com
thamesandhudsonusa.com
thamesandhudson.com.au